THE OLD CITY OF JERUSALEM May 28, 1948

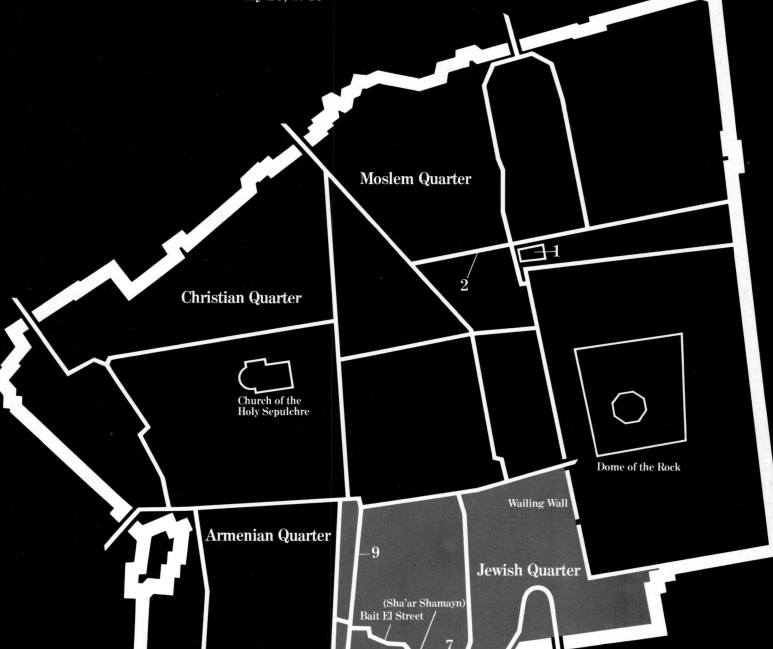

Moslem Quarter

Christian Quarter

Church of the
Holy Sepulchre

Dome of the Rock

Wailing Wall

Armenian Quarter

Jewish Quarter

9

(Sha'ar Shamayn)
Bait El Street

8
—
10

7

3

5

4

6

1 Major Tel's headquarters at the rauda
2 Tuval's journey down the Via Dolorosa
3 Rusnak's headquarters at the Batei Mahse
4 The two Rabbis at the Armenian Seminary
5 Rabbi Weingarten led to Seminary
6 Rusnak surrenders near Zion Gate
7 Prisoners lined up on Ashkenazi Square
8 Refugees herded past Rothschild House
9 Rachel escapes down The Street of the Jews (cover)
10 The last Jew in the Old City for 19 years

A WILL TO SURVIVE

A WILL TO SURVIVE

Text and Photographs by
John Phillips

Foreword by Golda Meir

Afterword by Teddy Kollek
(with J. Robert Moskin)

The Dial Press/James Wade
New York

Published by
The Dial Press/James Wade
1 Dag Hammarskjold Plaza
New York, New York 10017

Some of the photographs were first published in the
June 7, 1948, issue of *Life; Life Special Report: The Spirit
of Israel* (1973) by John Phillips, © Time Inc.; and the
April 3, 1976, issue of *Saturday Review*.

Manufactured in the United States of America

First softcover printing
Design by Massimo Vignelli
Production by Warren Wallerstein

A hardcover edition of this work is available through
The Dial Press.

Library of Congress Cataloging in Publication Data

Phillips, John, 1914–
    A will to survive.

    1.   Jerusalem – Siege, 1948 – Personal narratives.
2.   Phillips, John, 1914 –   I.   Title.
DS126.99.J4P48   956.94′4′05   77-2204
ISBN 0-8037-0176-4 (hardcover)
ISBN 0-8037-0182-9 (paperback)

Contents

Acknowledgments

At the invitation of Mayor Teddy Kollek, I returned to Jerusalem in 1975 to photograph the places and people I had photographed on my visit to the city in 1948. On this return visit the idea of a special exhibition of the photographs was born. The exhibition, which took place at the Israel Museum in the autumn of 1976 with the help of the Jerusalem Foundation, and my book are the results of that visit.

My warm appreciation goes to the organizers of the Israel Museum exhibition and to Mishkenot Sha'ananim for its kind hospitality.

My appreciation also goes to Ralph Baum of Modernage Photographic Services for his role as *shadchan*—matchmaker—when he brought Mayor Kollek and myself together.

I would like to take this opportunity to express my gratitude to Miss Margaret Weiss, whose article in the *Saturday Review* about the pictures that now appear in my book sparked a chain reaction of interest in this work.

I also wish to thank Lincoln Barnett, a friend from the days when we were both in the early stages of *Life*, for reading my manuscript and making constructive suggestions.

My thanks, too, to Don Seaman, a secretary who can work for hours without fatigue marring his elegant typewritten pages, for deferring all other commitments and returning to New York to assist me in this undertaking.

In addition, I wish to remember my friend, Tom Stone, a dark-room technician at the Time and Life Lab, for the enthusiasm with which he devoted his days off to work with me in my dark room. And I cannot forget Jorge Figueroa, from Modernage, for stunning blow-ups.

Finally, I must record my admiration for Anna Maria's great talent and tenacity in tracing survivors from the Old City of Jerusalem, and her patience in putting up with a husband who is not only a photo-journalist, but a Welshman with a low boiling point, and a Scorpio at that.

To those who died—
but not in vain.

A great deal in this book is universal; it is the tragedy of our century that we have had to look so often into the eyes of ordinary, confused and weary human beings who are frightened and in pain and who, through no fault of their own, have been forced to experience the terror of war. The tragedy that befell the men, women and children whom Mr. Phillips photographed and with whom he spoke in Jerusalem in the spring of 1948 has befallen millions throughout the world over the past five or six decades.

But the truth is that Israel's War of Independence was different from other wars, for had it been lost, nothing would have remained. The state itself was less than two weeks old when these heartbreaking photographs were taken in the besieged Jewish Quarter of the Old City. What hung in the balance during those few dreadful days was not only the fate of a handful of brave fighters or that of a tiny civilian population, but also the fate of a nation. Brought into existence after two thousand years, could it survive despite the overwhelming odds it faced and the unreasoning hostility into which it was born? However, the State of Israel endured. It grew and it prospered, and so, miraculously, this becomes a story with a happy ending: the record of a hard-won victory and of an ideal that prevailed because there were people who profoundly believed in it and because the need was so great. In fact, it is also something else: the story of the wonderful way in which Jerusalem—now freely shared by the three faiths to whom it is holy—has been rehabilitated and restored, and of the new life that has been carved from the rubble to which the quarter was once reduced.

My deepest hope, which, of course, I share with all Israelis, is that peace will come soon to my country and that we will, at last, be allowed to devote ourselves entirely to the purpose for which the State of Israel was created: developing the land for the good of all its inhabitants. That day may not yet be near, but when it dawns—as it surely will—this book may help to remind the world of the price that was paid for peace, who paid for it, who destroyed, and who rebuilt.

Golda Meir

Ramat Aviv,
September 1976

1

A Word of Explanation

The pictures I took in the Jewish Quarter of Jerusalem on May 28, 1948, during the Israeli War of Independence, have given rise to some questions I would like to answer.

People have expressed amazement that a Jew was able to photograph the plight of the Israelis in the aftermath of their surrender to the Arab Legion. What amazes me is that anyone would assume I must be Jewish to have taken "such compassionate pictures." No Jewish photographer could have shot the pictures I did. The rampaging Arabs would have killed him. Being a White Anglo-Saxon Protestant was no help either. Conditions were such that anyone with a camera was considered a Jewish spy and promptly set upon. I managed to get the pictures that illustrate this book only because I was in the uniform of the Arab Legion. Mistaking me for a British officer, the Arab populace left me alone—at first.

Aware that the sack of the Jewish Quarter would shock the western world, Arab authorities across the Middle East tried to prevent the news from leaking out. Jerusalem could not be mentioned under any circumstances. A dutiful Cairo censor even wanted to blue-pencil every reference to Jerusalem in the Bible of a departing tourist. I knew my pictures on the agony of the Jewish Quarter would end up in a censor's wastepaper basket. I did not want this to happen and decided to smuggle them out of the Middle East. There was some risk, but I took the chance. The record of what really happened in Old Jerusalem on May 28, 1948, was saved for posterity, should posterity care.

Why would a gentile become embroiled in such a conflict? I'd be lying if I sanctimoniously claimed that I was merely doing my job as a representative of the free press. Through happenstance I had spent most of my adult life recording violence, and editors were in the habit of assigning me to violent stories. I was particularly interested in this conflict because I was born in Algeria, grew up among Arabs and Jews, and have an affinity for both.

My Algerian upbringing taught me what it feels like to belong to a minority group. At the Petit Lycée Mustapha Supérieur in Algiers I found out what it meant to be called "a dirty Englishman," how lonely and desperate you feel when surrounded by a hostile crowd. I was held personally responsible for Joan of Arc going to the stake. "You burned our saint!" a wild-eyed French classmate screamed, kicking me in the face after I was down. The result was a broken nose and a lifelong sympathy for minorities.

In Algiers I learned how Arab hostility for the Jews was encouraged by French colonials. Politically Algeria was French territory; in fact it was as colonial as Palestine, where I had a chance to observe "the Palestine Problem" in 1943. In truth, the problem was a tragedy of promises made to two peoples that were never kept. By today's standards the Arabs and Jews were double-crossed. By the Victo-

2

rian criteria that guided colonial England, the political deception was considered perfectly legitimate, as it was performed in the name of King and Country. The origins of this tragedy, which has plagued the world for over half a century, lie in the Ottoman Empire's decision to side with Germany in World War I. British strategists in Cairo saw that the quickest way to knock Turkey out of the war was to encourage the Arab provinces, under Ottoman rule, to revolt. These provinces covered an expanse we now call Lebanon, Syria, Iraq, Jordan, Israel and Saudi Arabia, but at that time they had no national identities of their own. Palestine, for instance, was part of southern Syria and subdivided into three separate administrative districts. In T. E. Lawrence the British found the ideal man to sponsor, and then lead, the Arab revolt. The price Britain agreed to pay was independence for the Arab provinces.

In recognition of Dr. Chaim Weizmann's contribution to the Allied war effort in the chemistry of high explosives, Great Britain brought forth the controversial Balfour Declaration. British Foreign Secretary Arthur Balfour promised a National Home for the Jews in Palestine.

Overriding these two idealistic but loosely worded promises was a much more crisply spelled out secret deal between Britain and France in which both agreed to keep for themselves those Turkish provinces the Arabs considered Arab and the Jews their National Home. The French got Damascus. Britain took over Jerusalem and turned the newly reconstituted Palestine into a way station on the road to India.

Mandate authorities, anxious to maintain Palestine in the state of somnolence it had enjoyed since 1516, agreed with the Arab chieftains on the disadvantages of a Jewish National Home. Both feared the down-to-earth Zionists, realizing that the creation of a National Home would precipitate radical changes in a land congealed in its feudal past. It would breed unrest among the Moslem masses, still perfectly content with their dreary lot. Seeking Arab support, mandate officials attempted to appease the insatiable Haj Amin el Husseini, Grand Mufti of Jerusalem, at the expense of the Zionists. This policy encouraged increasing Arab violence, which culminated eventually in the Mufti defecting to Nazi Germany.

It took a world war to bring temporary peace to the Middle East and VE Day for renewed violence to erupt in Palestine. Desperate Jews there took the offensive. Unable to cope with the problem, Britain dropped Palestine into the UN's lap in 1947. The international wrangle that followed—leading to the fiercely debated resolution to partition Palestine into two independent states—illustrated once again the difficulties a country faces when situated at the crossroads of power politics.

The world powers, trailed by smaller nations, hoped to benefit from an Arab-Israeli conflict. Russia, eager to weaken Great Britain's influence in the Mideast, favored the partition plan spearheaded by the United States. The U.S., growing wary of Russia's intentions, tried to backtrack by advocating a "temporary trusteeship regime" for Palestine.

Determined to maintain some influence in the Middle East, Great Britain encouraged the Anglophile King Abdullah of Jordan to annex Arab Palestine with his British-trained legion.

France favored an Arab defeat, which would discourage Algerian, Moroccan and Tunisian claims for independence. Fearful of Moslem fanaticism, the Lebanese Christians regarded Arab antagonism for the Jews as a safety valve. Syria saw in the Arab-Israeli war a pretext to absorb Palestine into a "Greater Syria." King Farouk viewed the upcoming war as a God-sent opportunity for his subjects to fix on something other than himself to hate. The same held true for the Iraqi royal family. Even the Moslem Turks had a stake in the war. They prayed quietly for a Jewish victory because an Arab one would trigger Syrian territorial claims against themselves.

These machinations obscured the real issue: Feudal lords like the Grand Mufti had held back progress for centuries. Now they found themselves confronted with a new and powerful twentieth-century force from the West—the Jews. The Jews themselves were not coming to the Middle East as colonists but as settlers. A great change was bound to follow Partition whether the Arabs chose to accept it or not. After four wars there is still no peace in the Middle East. Foreign interference continues as in the past, Russia having replaced Great Britain. The Soviets have disrupted direct negotiations between the Arabs and Israelis by consistently re-arming the Arabs and encouraging yet another war.

The general public has come to believe that the Arabs and Israelis cannot live in peace together. This is not true. It is simply a matter of finding an Arab statesman who would dare what King Feisal attempted in 1919. Feisal, who with T. E. Lawrence had led the victorious Arab revolt, met with Chaim Weizmann at the Paris Peace Conference. They came to a visionary agreement based on "a most cordial good will between Arabs and Jews." Feisal would encourage Zionist immigration to Palestine; Weizmann promised Zionist assistance in Arab economic development. This agreement was signed on January 3, 1919, and was conditional on Arab independence being fulfilled. Soon after, the French expelled Feisal from Syria in accordance with their secret deal with Britain, while the British themselves retained Palestine. A chance for peace in the Middle East was lost. I believe this chance will come again.

The Road to the Old City

December 2, 1947, was one of those bleak autumn days you occasionally get in Rome. A threatening overcast had turned the gold ochre city to a dull grey. The lighting was flat and lifeless, just the kind of day a photographer dreads. Fortunately, I had no assignment that afternoon—or so I thought.

I was driving toward the Colosseum when I came upon people carrying banners. A crowd in the street during the Roman siesta was unusual enough to make me stop and take a look at this silent and orderly procession.

"Can't be a political rally," I reasoned. Such demonstrations were always noisy and held near the Chamber of Deputies, ringed by units of the *celere*—the anti-riot squads. But here there wasn't a policeman in sight. I watched crowds flow from side streets and merge into a single column at the Colosseum. There were no onlookers. I was sure it couldn't be a parade. It was Monday. In Italy a parade, like roast chicken, was a Sunday treat.

I was wrong. It was indeed a parade, and it had attracted Jewish people from all over Italy. I slung a camera over my shoulder and joined the marchers on the off chance something might develop. We set off toward the Roman Forum, straight for the Arch of Titus. Normally Jews never went there. This monument, glorifying the destruction of the Temple in Jerusalem, was for them a symbol of despair. But today it was different. The State of Israel had just been resurrected by the United Nations General Assembly.

We reached the arch, where a large wreath was inscribed: AFTER 1,877 YEARS THE JEWISH STATE REAPPEARS. "What a triumph for faith," I thought. This was a march across time—driven by a people's will to survive—which linked pre-Biblical times to the Atomic Age. It was like watching a legend come to life. Aware of being an intruder, I moved among these silent people at a moment awaited by their forebears for twenty tormented centuries. I searched for a look, a gesture, which would sum up this moment. All I could see was the blurry uniformity of an anonymous gathering. The emotions of these people ran too deep for my alien eyes.

A rabbi and three other speakers stood beneath the arch. The crowd gathered around to listen. In Italian, Hebrew and Yiddish, the speakers recalled the Jewish people's long history. It seemed more epitaph to a spent holocaust than a celebration over the birth of a nation.

A voice said: "You didn't destroy the Jewish state, Titus. You Romans conquered the world but one nation never bowed to your rule—the Jews. We revolted three times. Each time you defeated us. The last time was in the year 78, but we still went on. Today we place our flag on your triumphal arch, Titus, to show that you were not victorious. Who put up the flag? A Jew like me. The offspring of some captive you brought to Rome in slavery. For almost two thousand years our people have kept alive the idea of Jewish existence."

In the back of everyone's mind was the thought that the Arabs had announced their intention of driving the Jews into the sea. Scattered fighting had already broken out. Barricades had been set up at Jaffa Gate to besiege the Jewish Quarter in Jerusalem. Two buses had been ambushed in an orange grove near Tel Aviv and the passengers killed. Arab convicts in Acre jail, responding to the Grand Mufti's florid battle cry—"When the sword speaks all else must remain silent"—had set upon their Jewish cellmates and started a prison riot. It was clear that the Israeli state, brought to life in Flushing Meadow, New York, must seek survival on Palestinian battlefields. Once more the Jews were on the march. This time it would be along rocky roads beneath a glaring sun where a hardy cactus grows—a cactus that had given its name to Jews born in Palestine—the Sabra. I knew these people to be tough, but wondered whether 600,000 Jews could hold off 30,000,000 Arabs.

At dusk the ceremony at the Arch of Titus came to an end. Before we went our separate ways I had a last look at a bas relief on the arch, which showed Roman soldiers making off with the menorah. How could I guess I would soon be photographing similar scenes?

In late February I was back in the Middle East searching for the elusive Haj Amin el Husseini, the Grand Mufti of Jerusalem, who was said to be in Cairo. I had been assigned to photograph the Mufti, because he was still the unchallenged leader of the Palestinian Arabs.

Haj Amin belonged to the el Husseini tribe, one of the two most influential Arab families in Palestine. Unlike their hated rivals, the Nashashibi, the Husseinis were not moderates. In time Haj Amin, who had as little use for Arab moderates as for Zionists, killed off his opposition, who numbered in the hundreds.

In the early twenties Herbert Samuel, Britain's first high commissioner to Palestine, decided to play the Husseini clan against their rivals, who controlled Jerusalem's town hall. He made Haj Amin the Mufti of Jerusalem, even though he did not qualify for this religious position since he had failed to pass his examination in Islamic philosophy at the Azhar University in Cairo. Soon after el Husseini became Palestine's religious leader, the high commissioner bolstered Haj Amin's spiritual standing by appointing him president of the Supreme Moslem Council with complete control of $400,000 in religious funds annually. Little did the high commissioner suspect he had advanced the career of Palestine's most implacable anti-Zionist. Strange as it may seem, Herbert Samuel was a Jew.

The Mufti parlayed his religious authority and financial power into a political machine so potent that Palestine was kept in turmoil for almost thirty years, and Jewish immigration virtually ground to a halt, before he fled to Germany and collaborated with the Nazis during World War II.

The years the Mufti had spent in Berlin had only increased his prestige among the Arabs. A most artful dodger, "der Grossmufti" had slipped out of Berlin on VE Day to reappear in France, confident he would never be brought to trial as a war criminal. He was not mistaken. DeGaulle's provisional government, mindful of his popularity among the North African Moslems under French rule, put him up in a villa near Paris while he was ostensibly waiting to be extradited to England for war crimes. Taking into consideration the consequences in Palestine if they tried and hanged the Mufti, the British did nothing to disturb his French sojourn, which lasted until June of 1946.

The Mufti then vanished from his Paris residence and resurfaced in Egypt as a guest of King Farouk, who had provided him with a villa behind high walls in Heliopolis on the outskirts of Cairo. The entire neighborhood was patrolled by Egyptian soldiers, but the suspicious Mufti preferred to rely on six burly Palestinian bodyguards who never left his side. Such was the man I hoped to photograph.

Word had it that the Mufti was in Beirut preparing to assume power in Palestine after the British mandate came to an end at midnight on May 14, 1948. The war was scheduled for Saturday, May 15, at dawn. I was wondering how to make contact with "Mr. Palestine," as the American press now called the Mufti, when I got a tip: Attend the seventh meeting of the Arab League Council at the Ministry of Foreign Affairs in Cairo.

As I approached the Foreign Office I was struck by the architecture—it suggested some sort of rich Oriental pastry. Its grandiose staircase and enormous rooms were laden with elaborate cream-colored cornices and chocolate colonnades. The furnishings matched the setting. So did the delegates, who came from Egypt, Iraq, Lebanon, Saudi Arabia, Syria, Trans-Jordan and Yemen. They wore cloaks in rich brocade, embroidered sashes with curved daggers of gold, nonchalantly draped *kouffiehs*, bright red tarbooshes with long tassels, fluffy turbans, and even western clothes with stiff wing collars, waistcoats and striped socks.

There was an air of anticipation as the delegates gathered in small groups earnestly—almost conspiratorially—conversing. All awaited the Mufti's arrival. Without warning he swept into the room, trailed by a respectful retinue. Never before had I seen such blatant self-assurance. The Mufti wore a flowing black robe with a gold brocade border and shiny patent leather shoes. His distinctive tarboosh, shaped like a flower pot, was planted firmly on his head. His hair was ginger, but white bristles flecked his neatly trimmed goatee. Unlike most Arabs, he did not gesture with his hands. He held them behind his back, thus conveying a thoughtful mien. I found his face extremely expressive as he moved briskly among the delegates. He had a warm, disarming smile which made him look like a mischievous child until you noticed the eyes—a cold cobalt blue. A member of his entourage came over to me. Wasn't I the cameraman who had photographed Jewish Palestine in 1943? Flattered that someone remembered the pictures I had taken for *Life*, I readily agreed. "And you have the audacity to appear in front of the Mufti after photographing Ben-Gurion?" he screamed.

A few days later I left for Damascus to look up the field commander of the Arab Liberation Army, which was now being recruited to fight in Palestine. His name was Fawzi el Kaoukji, affectionately called the Lion of Damascus. A fellow conspirator of the Mufti's, the Lion had joined him in Berlin during World War II. Less fortunate than Haj Amin in making his getaway after Germany's defeat, Fawzi had been captured by the Russians and sent to a concentration camp until Syria requested his release.
Fawzi's career was the kind of political maze only an Arab nationalist can stumble through. Born in Lebanon, he served in the Turkish army during the First World War. That he had fought against the French did not prevent Fawzi from joining their Special Forces when they took over Syria in 1920. And being a French officer did not prevent him from plotting against them by joining the fierce Djebel Druze tribesmen when they rebelled against France in 1926. After their defeat Fawzi fled to Saudi Arabia, then moved on to Iraq in 1928. At the invitation of the commander of the Iraqi general staff, Fawzi became an instructor at their military school. That did not prevent him from joining a pro-German revolt against the pro-British government he was serving. In the winter of 1948 he assumed field command of the Arab Liberation Army. His commander-in-chief was none other than the Iraqi general he had betrayed in 1941.
Although Fawzi was in Damascus, I soon found out that, while everybody knew he was in town, nobody was willing to mention his whereabouts. "Remember, the British still have a price on his head," was the reply whenever I made a point of finding the Lion. Though Fawzi kept out of sight, his presence was keenly felt. Damascus was, after all, the headquarters of the Arab drive against Zionism.
Recruiting posters were displayed all over town. Exhortations to enlist were flashed on movie screens and heard over the radio. Contributions to the war effort were solicited on the street, in the schools, and even in the courtyards of the Umyyad Mosque, where John the Baptist's head is buried. Slogans in squiggly Arab script were displayed everywhere. The mildest of them warned: "You who want to build a nation over our bodies are building on a volcano." Recruits in their black-and-white checkered *kouffiehs* crowded the streets. Although the Liberation Army had MPs to keep the volunteers in line, the recruits

were bold enough to try and commandeer my car on Hedjaz Avenue as I was following up a lead on Fawzi's hideout. Without bothering to open the door, they tried to haul me out of the car window. My muffled howls attracted several officers who casually booted their recruits out of the way and advised me to drive on.
This was nothing compared to the Rally of Emancipated Moslem Women I attended on the off chance Fawzi might show up. Frenzy overcame the audience after a bucket of Palestinian sand was produced and ceremoniously passed around for all to dip their fingers into. Om Shouaid Dandachi, a fat lady in a flowing purple gown with a large white muslin bow covering layers of double chins, was the main speaker.
"I can't wait to drink blood from the skulls of Jews I'm going to kill in Palestine!" she told her ecstatic listeners. As I was standing near her taking pictures, she grabbed my tie and yanked it to show her contempt for American aid to the Jews. Public humiliation by a woman in this charged atmosphere could prove disastrous for me. Casually I raised a hand to my neck as if to straighten my tie and seized the little finger of her right hand. Folding it at the joint, I held it between my thumb and forefinger like a nutcracker. Without taking my eyes off her, I squeezed. She let go. I jumped back and reached for an army rifle which I handed to her, saying, "Please hold it with both hands." As she stood grimly at the ready, I hurriedly took her picture and decamped.
A few days later, in hopes of obtaining an introduction to Fawzi, I visited Syria's minister of defense, but got nowhere. "Just wait and see," the minister advised me.
So I waited.
Quite by chance I had a drink with Fawzi's executive officer at the bar of the Orient Palace Hotel. After the third *rakkia*—a Middle Eastern version of absinthe—he promised to arrange a meeting with Fawzi.
The Lion's den was on the ground floor of a modern apartment house. His child's diapers were strung out on clotheslines in the courtyard to dry. Ducking beneath them, I came face to face with Fawzi. "I'm not a man of words," the Lion roared. "I'm a man of action. And the time for deeds is near!"
"How near?" I asked.
"Just wait and see," Fawzi said.
So I waited.
Early in March I got word that Fawzi was ready to move into Palestine. For security reasons he would not allow me to go along with him, but I was permitted to photograph his departure. Before leaving, his executive officer told me to contact Sabri Pasha Taba, Fawzi's man in Trans-Jordan.
Glowingly described to me as a Moslem with the grace and hospitality of a Bedouin uncontaminated by western civilization, Sabri Pasha Taba received me in his Amman warehouse smoking a *nargileh* and

seated among bales of rice. He offered me the traditional three cups of Turkish coffee, but declined to issue a *laissez passer* to Fawzi's headquarters, its location kept secret on grounds of national security. "Just wait and see," he said encouragingly.

So I waited.

In spite of all this secrecy it was common knowledge that Fawzi was at Jaba in Samaria. Two Jewish planes had dropped four antipersonnel bombs on the Lion's command post the day before I drove there without military clearance.

Fawzi did not seem surprised to see me. He put on his sun helmet, picked up his binoculars, and led me to a veranda where shriveled geraniums drooped in gasoline cans beneath a hot sun. Studying the hills, olive groves, cacti, rocks and dust of northern Palestine, he announced: "The time for deeds has come!"

Then he took me to lunch.

Seated at Fawzi's table were his Lebanese dentist and his doctor, in the company of Iraqi, Palestinian and Syrian officers. There was a brutishness about the way they roared with laughter and slapped their thighs in delight at the prospect of wallowing in Jewish blood. It was as if their natural habitat were the sixteenth century. I was reminded of my school days in France when we were taught about the ferocious mercenaries who looted cities and put their enemies to the sword. I find it impossible to judge these men in contemporary terms and can still recall, as though it were today, the anachronistic emotions I felt while among these feudal warriors laden down with modern weapons. My impression was shared by a Yugoslav volunteer I met after lunch. "What rabble!" he said contemptuously. "They have no idea what a real fighting outfit is like. I do. I was with the Waffen S.S."

From him I learned that Fawzi's strategy was to besiege Jerusalem and starve out its inhabitants by the end of the mandate. Although I grasped Fawzi's grand design, I could not understand why his forces always made a wide detour over very bad roads to avoid the Jewish settlements that controlled the main road to Jerusalem.

"You want to know why Fawzi doesn't attack those two settlements?" the former S.S. growled. "Just wait and see."

I found out in Haifa. Three weeks before the mandate ended the Haganah took the calculated risk that British Royal Marines stationed there would not defend the harbor. The Haganah seized this chance to avoid being cut off from their supply lines once the fighting began in earnest. Surrounded on all sides by Arab forces supplied by overland routes, the Israelis would have to rely on shipping. With the only docking facilities concentrated in Haifa, it was imperative to gain control of the port by evicting the Arab population. The Haganah gambled on the British government not risking heavy casualties to defend a harbor they were soon to evacuate. The gamble paid off. Notified of the Israeli plan, the British command

pulled back their marines to within the dock area. By the time I got to Haifa the main objectives were in Jewish hands. The city was silent, its 65,000 Arab refugees stunned and speechless. They tramped toward the docks and were evacuated by the British to Acre across the bay. I was photographing these refugees as they limped past when a young Jewish commando called out, "Remember, we had to leave Egypt two thousand years ago!"

Violence and terror increased steadily as May 15 drew near. Weapons were peddled on Arab street corners as though they were Jaffa oranges. British deserters, German S.S., Polish and Yugoslav mercenaries hired by the Arabs performed acts of sabotage. The Irgun and the Stern Gang retaliated. The more enlightened Arabs began to have doubts about Jews being the cringing cowards they had always imagined. Defeat was in the air. Panic struck the Palestinian Arab population. Over 200,000 abandoned their homes and took to the roads leading to Amman. Down to Jericho and the Dead Sea they streamed, spreading wild rumors to justify their flight. Plump city fathers, escorted by bodyguards, hastened to Jordan to seek King Abdullah's help.

It must have been devastating for the Mufti to contemplate failure just when he expected to reap the rewards of his life's ambition. At the very moment his Arab Charter for Palestine was submitted to the UN Security Council, he found himself without military backing. The one force he had counted on—the Arab Liberation Army—had fared badly whenever it tangled with the Jews, in spite of overwhelming numerical superiority. Whatever effectiveness this motley force might once have had was greatly reduced through treachery and corruption.

Arab Liberation Army officers sold their military equipment to the Israelis. Funds raised for the war chests were converted into bullion by venal ministers. Abdel Kader el Husseini, a faithful cousin of the Mufti's and the most popular Arab commander in Palestine, had been killed in a skirmish. Distrust between the Mufti and Fawzi turned to bad blood. An observer overheard Fawzi berate his old Berlin associate, roaring, "*Du bist ein Schweinehund*, Mufti!" What must have made failure even more galling to the Mufti was that power had now passed to his arch enemy, the king of Jordan. King Abdullah was a brother of the late Feisal, who had led the Arab revolt with Lawrence, liberated Damascus, and had subsequently been expelled from Syria by the French in accordance with the secret Franco-British agreement. Like Feisal, Abdullah was a moderate by Moslem standards. For the Arabs this monarch, with his British-trained army, was their only hope.

Early in May I went to Amman and visited King Abdullah. He posed for me in a gleaming white Bedouin costume, his Hedjazi turban worn at a rakish angle. Abdullah was tiny. Yet he conveyed dignity through his bearing and distinguished features. His skin was as smooth as a baby's and as dark as a

Havana cigar. His black eyes sparkled. A carefully trimmed beard gave him an air of severity, dispelled occasionally by an impish smile.

At lunch Abdullah told me, "I am an Arab king of an Arab state with an Arab army. I shall do as I please!"

"What Abdullah really wants to do," the French ambassador said to me later, "is play both Saladin and Richard the Lion-Hearted in this twentieth-century crusade."

In other words Abdullah intended to play both ends against the middle by appearing to champion blind Arab nationalism while accepting the inevitability of Partition at the same time. Abdullah would not squander his legion in a costly war against the Israelis. The western world would recognize his moderation and statesmanship. The United States would most certainly recognize his kingdom. He would continue to benefit from British aid while also acquiring Arab Palestine.

The Mufti fully realized all the advantages Abdullah would derive from moderation, and suspected him of such treachery. This suspicion was not restricted to the Mufti, the Egyptians, Iraqis, Lebanese, Syrians or the Saudis. It was felt also by Abdullah's own Bedouins and even his oldest son, Crown Prince Emir Talal, who objected to his father's policy as an Arab patriot.

"You talk of patriotism," Abdullah screamed at the crown prince, "but you don't know a thing about it! We need a strong ally. Russia is out of the question. America isn't interested. Only the British know us well enough to help, even though they've let us down in the past."

The break between father and son was a breach between two generations of Arabs. Abdullah believed in benevolent despotism backed by a strong western power. His son wanted Arab independence without foreign domination. While Abdullah saw the approaching war as an opportunity to extend the boundaries of his kingdom, his son saw it as an expression of pan-Arabism. Abdullah schemed in terms of power politics; his son dreamed of the Arab emancipation to come.

On May 14 the stage was set. Early that morning Sir Alan Cunningham, the British high commissioner, left Government House on the Hill of Evil Counsel outside Jerusalem to the mournful sound of Scottish bagpipes. Sir Alan was driven to Kalandia Airport in a bulletproof Daimler. On landing in Haifa he boarded the cruiser HMS *Euryalus* as the band struck up "The Minstrel Boy." At the stroke of midnight HMS *Euryalus*, floodlit by the searchlights of her destroyer escorts, crossed the three-mile limit into international waters. The British mandate in Palestine had ended. The State of Israel was born. The war could now begin.

All that day Arab Legion units moved down into the valley of Jericho, where they bivouacked. Wearing a new khaki uniform made by his Armenian tailor, King Abdullah watched his Bedouin warriors per-

form a wild war dance, pigtails flying. At dawn the Arab Legion crossed Allenby Bridge and entered Palestine.

Accredited to the legion, I tagged along. For the first time since late February I had no fear that some paranoid Moslem would try to lynch me for taking pictures. I was in the legion uniform and treated with respect by the populace, who mistook me for a British officer serving in the Arab army. By nightfall the legion had taken up defensive positions in Palestine. I decided to see what Fawzi's irregulars were up to. Their objective was to take the settlements of Atarot and Neve Yaacov which controlled the road to Jerusalem—the two Fawzi had been avoiding when I last saw him. Atarot lay near Kalandia Airport, from where Sir Alan had left Jerusalem. The *kibbutz* had been evacuated on the night of the fifteenth by its garrison.

By the time I got there only smouldering ruins remained. Airmail letters from the States and sheet music from Mozart's *Magic Flute* were scattered around. Most of the Holstein cows left behind had been killed by the Liberation Army to prevent the Arabs from fighting over them.

From Atarot I pushed on to Neve Yaacov. This settlement was built on a rise and the Arab objective was the fortified school used as a blockhouse. Arab artillerymen fired at least thirty shells while I stood by. Not one hit its mark. All landed on the other side of the hill where, I was told, there was an Arab village.

That night the garrison at Neve Yaacov pulled out. The next morning I came upon a group of British deserters. "We're what you might call 'unofficial transfers' to Fawzi's army," their spokesman, a Scot named Tich, explained with a wink as the group stood at the entrance of the settlement. Turning, he shouted to the Arab constables who were beating off impatient looters, "Keep the buggers off, mon, the whole bloody place is mined!" Then he calmly removed the fuse from a milk churn crammed with nuts and bolts.

"Keep that bugger away! He's going to get his balls blown off!" Tich warned as an impatient Arab clawed his way past a guard. There was a bang and a howl. A hush came over the crowd as the wounded Arab was carted off.

"That'll keep the buggers quiet," Tich grinned.

I watched the deserters as they efficiently defused mines and booby traps. One of them was a German, a twenty-one-year-old S.S. who had escaped from a French POW camp. After Neve Yaacov was demined, the men decided to move on before the Arabs ran wild.

Tich briefed me on the situation in the Old City of Jerusalem before I headed there. A unit of Fawzi's irregulars were besieging the Jewish Quarter.

"It's a piece of cake, mon," Tich said, explaining that the quarter was cut off from the New City—in Israeli hands—by the towering wall started by Solomon and completed by Saladin. The Jews were hemmed in by the Armenian, Christian and Moslem quarters and, as if that were not enough, the Jewish Quarter had been besieged by the Arabs since Partition was announced in late November 1947, preventing the Haganah from sending in help.

"The Jews are balmy to hang onto that pile of stone," Tich said.

I knew enough about the Haganah to realize that, while the old quarter might well be indefensible, they would defend it. This was the Jerusalem that Jewish people around the world asked to return to in their prayers.

I drove to the Old City via Jericho. On reaching the Mount of Olives I came to a sweeping bend in the road. The New City—a shimmering peach color under a blazing sun—was spread out before me. An armored car was firing into the city while a large Arab crowd watched the shelling with obvious satisfaction. No sooner had I joined them than a sharp crack was heard, like that of a walnut being split open. I dived for cover even before I spotted the Arab who had been hit in the head.

Dusting myself off, I entered the Old City on foot, passing through Saint Stephen's Gate. I was in search of Arab Legion headquarters, set up in the *rauda*—a Moslem kindergarten located at the First Station of the Cross, where Pontius Pilate sentenced Jesus to be crucified.

Major Tel was in command of the Arab Legion forces in the Old City. In civilian clothes he would have passed unnoticed in the city of London. His moustache was very British, as was his self-control. With him was Dr. Mousa el Husseini, suave nephew of the Mufti and civilian Arab representative. In appearance these two had little in common with Arabs who milled around—excitable members of Egypt's Moslem Brotherhood wearing bandoliers, swashbuckling Iraqi irregular officers in *kouffiehs* draped like turbans, and pudgy city fathers from Amman who kept asking anxiously about the progress of the war. In the midst of this hubbub Turkish coffee was being served and the phone rang incessantly. More often than not the call was from King Abdullah. Major Tel would stand up, wearily order silence, and inform his monarch that the Jews were still holding out in the Old City.

I got some idea of how this operation was going when a British deserter reported to Major Tel about a synagogue under attack. It was so jammed with irregulars busy looting, there wasn't any elbow room to fight off an Israeli counterattack.

"Something must be done," he told the major before turning to me and adding, "You should see the silly bastards."

With the deserter as a guide, I got my first look at the Jewish Quarter under fire (overleaf). From a spot near the Wailing Wall I could see Porat Josef synagogue rising in the distance across no-man's-land. The synagogue, with its adjoining Talmudic schools and academy, was disintegrating behind billows of smoke. The massive walls were coming down in a rising torrent of stone debris. Stunned by this spectacle of wanton destruction, I wondered just how many tons of TNT the Arab Liberation Army would squander to reduce this seat of learning to dust. For the next eleven days, recording the destruction of the Jewish Quarter was to be my life.

The Fall of the City

A pink bromeliad bloomed in an old gasoline can on the window ledge. From behind it two Arab irregulars fired away. A third jammed a fresh clip into his rifle. A fourth was slumped on a chair, sound asleep. I had no idea where I was. The British deserter, whom I had met at the *rauda* when he was complaining about looters in the synagogues, had led me here via a zigzag course from legion headquarters. Hurrying down narrow streets, we had passed barbwire entanglements at intersections guarded by tense, brooding irregulars. We had crawled over the rubble of houses, which had collapsed into the streets, and trudged through mounds of debris—ankle deep in broken furniture, piles of newspaper, rags and smashed crockery. We had ducked beneath low archways and sneaked from one building to another through gaping holes in the walls. Whenever we paused to catch our breath, all I seemed to see were damaged synagogues. "They must have at least fifty, and every one is a fortress," the deserter had said in disgust.

Now, with no more idea of what the irregulars were shooting at than of my bearings, I asked if I could look out the window. Obligingly one of them stepped aside. There in front of me rose a massive synagogue, awesome in its proportions and the extent of its damage. I was now contemplating the famous Hurva, which means "the Ruin" (opposite page). Renowned as the most striking edifice in all of Palestine, this synagogue had earned its name during the century and a half it had stood neglected between the laying of its foundations and its completion. Now, once again, the Hurva was a ruin.

It must have been May 19th that I became aware of Arab Legion *jundis* in full battle dress streaming into the Old City. Something was up, but nobody was talking. I finally heard the news from the British deserter.

On the night of the 18th the Haganah had broken through Zion Gate and reopened communication with the besieged Jewish Quarter for a few hours. They had brought in medical supplies, ammunition and reinforcements. Glubb Pasha, the British commander-in-chief of the Arab Legion, was convinced that the irregulars could not stop the Israelis from taking over all of the Old City and decided to commit the legion, which until then was being held in

reserve. These fierce Bedouins had nothing in common with the ineffectual Liberation Army. They were highly trained, well disciplined and fully equipped.

The Israelis had a fight on their hands. For ten days and nights the battle raged. By day the Arabs blasted their way into the Jewish Quarter with their artillery. At night the peaceful beauty of a moon over Jerusalem was clawed by red tracers spattering across the sky like streaks of blood. From time to time I heard a woman's scream above the roar of gunfire. On May 28 the exhausted Israeli fighters surrendered. The incessant gunfire echoing within the walled city had numbed my mind. I was filthy from

crawling around in the dust and had contracted dysentery. After the electric power failed, I did not know whether to feel ashamed of myself or blame the war when I walked into the Church of the Holy Sepulchre and appropriated a candle to help me find my way around the Austrian Hospice where I was lodged.

Shortly after nine on the morning of May 28 I went to
the Arab Legion's advance post in the Armenian
Quarter. The cease-fire was in effect. A feeling of
excitement prevailed among the men gathered
around the monastery courtyard.

"The Jews want to surrender," a legion officer said.
"They've sent over two rabbis." I found them seated
on a bench next to an MP. On the left, in a black felt
hat, was Rabbi Mintzberg, an Ashkenazi who represented the European community. He seemed lost in
prayer.

Rabbi Hazan wore a red tarboosh draped in black
cloth. A Sephardic, he represented the Oriental community. A ricochet had grazed his face while he was
making his way from the Jewish positions to the
forward Arab lines. Unmindful of his wound, he
stared with patriarchal intensity at Major Tel, who
was on the phone.

Major Tel must have been receiving orders from
Glubb Pasha in Amman. "I will only negotiate with a
member of the Israeli army," he told the rabbis after
he put down the receiver. Rabbi Hazan set off for the
Jewish lines with the major's demand, while Rabbi
Mintzberg remained in the Armenian Quarter.
Curious about the Arabs' reaction to him, I followed
Rabbi Hazan outside. Several grinned broadly. Oth-
ers watched solemnly as the rabbi majestically
descended the stairs. Not one appeared hostile.

"Here comes Mayor Weingarten!" a legionnaire announced, heralding the arrival of the spokesman for the Jewish community in the Old City. I wondered why he had come when Major Tel had expressly stated he would only negotiate with a representative of the army. A group of six escorted Mordechai Weingarten along the alleyway leading to the Armenian monastery. One was an Arab Legion officer; the others I guessed by their motley uniforms to be from the Liberation Army.

To my surprise the legionnaire held Weingarten's right hand—a friendly gesture among Moslems. The Arab on Weingarten's left held his arm with a certain diffidence. Although it was a hot day Mr. Weingarten wore an overcoat, presumably to add dignity to his person.

What had happened to the Haganah representative, the one I was really interested in photographing? Unfortunately I could not locate Major Tel to find out, and no one around me was helpful. Taking a chance that Major Tel was at his headquarters in the *rauda*, I crossed the Old City on foot to see what I could learn.

It must have been noon when I got to the *rauda*. Major Tel was not there. I was wondering what to do next when I heard the sound of an approaching crowd. A group of irregulars was coming down the Via Dolorosa. They had an Israeli in custody. I got a close-up shot of the prisoner and his guards. The Israeli looked apprehensive. I could not blame him, considering the murderous mood of the Arab civilians.

Once inside the *rauda*, the prisoner relaxed somewhat. He identified himself as Tawil, the military representative sent to negotiate with Major Tel. Escaping the attention of the press, Major Tel had already seen Tawil in the Armenian Quarter and laid down his terms. While on his way back to the Israeli lines Tawil had been set upon by two Arab irregulars. Flushed with victory at having captured the first Jewish prisoner in the Old City, the pair had refused to believe Tawil's explanation that he had just seen Major Tel in the Armenian Quarter. In spite of his protests, they had marched their prisoner across the Old City to the *rauda*. Leaving Tawil there, I hurriedly returned to the Armenian Quarter in search of Major Tel.

I arrived back at the Armenian monastery in time to photograph the Israeli delegation leaving for the Jewish lines under the watchful eye of an Arab Legion MP who kept his hand on a grenade. Tawil, the Haganah negotiator I had left behind at the *rauda*, was now with the group, having been returned in an Arab Legion vehicle. Major Tel reappeared to announce that fighting had ceased and the surrender would be signed at 4:00 P.M.

At a quarter to four I set out with a group of correspondents down Armenian Orthodox Patriarchate Road to Zion Gate, where the Haganah had broken through on the night of May 18 and where the surrender was now to be signed. The terms had originally been drawn up in Arabic, but both sides agreed on English as a common language. A Lebanese correspondent translated the terms into English. A copy for each side was written out in long hand by Don Burke, of *Time* magazine, using my pen. There was only one modification of the terms in the translation. In the original Arabic it had been stated that "all able-bodied men" would be treated as prisoners of war. This was changed to read "all fighters," with Major Tel to make the final decision on those who were fighters and those who were not.

The Israeli signatories were Mayor Mordechai Weingarten and Moshe Rusnak, military commander of the Jewish Quarter. While the somber young officer signed, Mousa el Husseini, a nephew of the Mufti and his representative in the Old City, looked on condescendingly. El Husseini then signed for the Arabs, followed by Major Tel. This formality was witnessed by Dr. Pablo de Azcarate, head of the United Nations Security Council Truce Commission. I glanced at my watch. It was exactly 4:36 P.M. on May 28, 1948.

Twenty-eight years later, two scenes still linger in my mind. . . .

The victor: Major Abdullah Tel contemplating the golden domed Mosque of Omar through a black wrought-iron grill at his headquarters in the *rauda* just before entering the Jewish Quarter.

The vanquished: The inhabitants of Batei Mahse awaiting their fate during the brief lull between the surrender and its aftermath.

Major Tel, with the signed surrender document in his hand, entered the small enclave still held by the Israelis. Mousa el Husseini, wearing a white linen jacket, along with Tawil, in shorts, and Moshe Rusnak, with an Eisenhower jacket slung over his shoulder, walked a step behind.

The Haganah fighters were drawn up in loose formation on Ashkenazi Square. They wore the vacant look of men who had been under constant fire and had slept little. Nothing about them revealed the fierce tenacity with which they had withstood the all-out attacks of the Arab Legion for ten days and nights.

There was one prisoner who especially aroused my curiosity. He was a British soldier who had joined the Haganah. I'd heard about him from one of his compatriots—the latter a pro-Arab deserter whom I shall call "Peter."

I had got to know Peter as he guided me around the maze of the Old City. Peter had been with the British army in Jerusalem for several years before he deserted, and he knew his way around. On the darkest night he prowled through the rubble, light-footed as a cat. There was also something feline about the way he stared through half-closed eyes. He always carried his rifle slung over his shoulder. I never saw him eat. He would abruptly disappear for a day or two and then reappear as unexpectedly, without a word of explanation.

One morning we were crawling across a roof which overlooked Israeli territory when Peter said, "The Arabs have had it. I have to get out of here fast. For that I need money, so I'll sell you my story."

Intent on taking pictures, I nodded without giving much thought to what he had said.

"It's going to cost you plenty," Peter went on, "because the money has got to take me someplace where the Jews can't get at me." There was desperation in his voice. "You see, I pulled the Ben Yehuda job."

This confession made me sit up momentarily until I realized I had become an Israeli target. "Is that the story you want to sell me, Peter?" I asked.

He nodded. "Yesterday I saw the Mufti in Damascus. He refused to pay me the five hundred pounds he had promised for the Ben Yehuda job, so I told him I'd sell you the story."

"Peter," I said, "over fifty people were killed when that truck loaded with explosives went up on Ben Yehuda Street. You wounded at least as many and flattened a couple of buildings. How do you expect any magazine to buy such a story?"

Two days later I received a visit from one of the Mufti's bodyguards. He was short, massive, and wore an astrakhan hat on the back of his head. His hands were square, his little finger the size of my thumb. He cracked his knuckles continually. "Some people talk too much," he told me. "Take Peter. The things he says." He rolled his eyes. Crack went his knuckles. "Give Peter a little advice. Just tell him writing can be even more unhealthy than talking." He turned and walked away, cracking his knuckles.

I didn't see Peter again until the Israelis surrendered. "There's a deserter from the Suffolk regiment who's with the Jews and I'm out to get the bugger," he told me. "His name's Albert Melville." When we reached Ashkenazi Square, Peter made straight for the group of prisoners. He looked them over carefully and exclaimed, "There's the bastard!" He was eyeing a man in a Haganah cap.

The man in the cap looked at me anxiously. "Sir," he said in a soft voice, "I didn't mean to desert, really I didn't. I got a bit squiffy one night in the Jewish Quarter, and when I sobered up I found I couldn't get out of here."

Peter grinned.

"I think they plan to shoot me, sir, and I didn't really mean to desert."

Peter grinned again.

I drew Major Tel's attention to the Englishman by asking what would happen to him. Tel assured me he would be treated like all the other prisoners of war. He would be transferred that night to an internment camp in Jordan.

Some days after the Israeli prisoners had reached Jordan, I made inquiries about him to the Jordanian authorities. He had never reached the POW camp. Nobody had ever heard of a British deserter. He had vanished without a trace.

So had Peter.

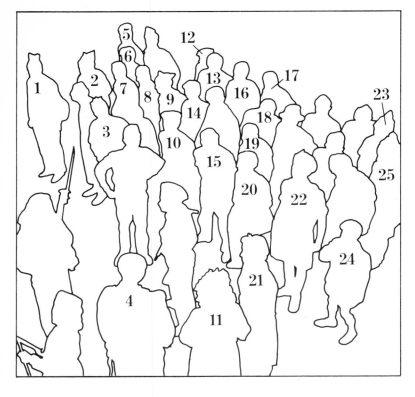

The Israeli prisoners in this picture, taken in Ashkenazi Square at the time of the surrender, are:

1) Moshe Yabrov	page	166
2) Zidkyahu Michaeli	page	148
3) Yaacov Kastel	page	118
4) Moshe Rusnak	page	116
5) Shimon Levy	page	110
6) Moshe Hasson	page	150
7) Menahem Waxman	page	186
8) Benjamin Yanir	page	140
9) Hevel S. Carmy	page	67
10) Moreno Mizrachi	page	104
11) Judith Kammar	page	108
12) Uri Sigawi	page	80
13) Shimon Benshemesh	page	128
14) Uri Golani	page	82
15) Joseph "Skip" Dahan	page	154
16) Asher Zedira	page	64
17) Yaacov Ben Rubi	page	158
18) Yehoshua Levy	page	122
19) Israel Philipp	page	100
20) Joseph Attieh	page	92
21) Malca Shimoni Dash	page	160
22) Joseph Almog	page	182
23) Avraham Weinfeld	page	86
24) Meir Alcotzer	page	74
25) Leonard Binder	page	176

The prisoners of war were marched off to the *kishleh*, an ancient Turkish prison near Jaffa Gate. There was some irony in the names of the streets along their route. Leaving Rothschild House behind, they went down Sha'ar Hashamyin—Gate of Heaven Road—which led them into Beit El—House of the Lord Street. On Rehov Ha Yehudim—the Street of the Jews—the procession halted while the legion cleared away hostile Arab civilians who blocked the way to the *kishleh*, where the prisoners would spend the night before being transported to an internment camp in Jordan.

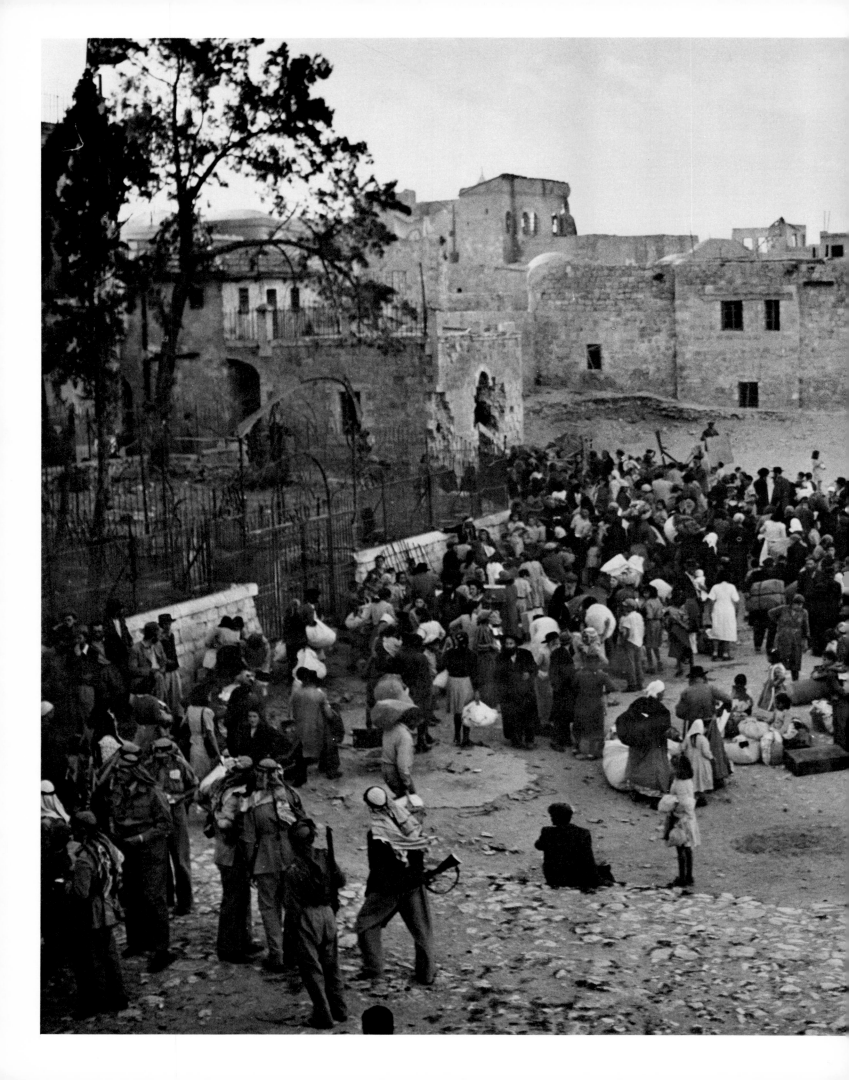

According to clause five of the surrender terms, civilians who elected to remain in the Jewish Quarter were free to do so on condition they recognized the sovereignty of King Abdullah. As far as I know, this clause was never invoked. In any case it could not have been enforced. Had any Jew decided to remain in the Old City he would have been homeless within hours and probably dead by nightfall.

Most of these civilians were Orthodox Jews. The men wore beards and side curls, wide-brimmed black felt hats and long black coats. The women wore babushkas. They were descendants of families that had lived in the Jewish Quarter for centuries. Now they had just one hour to pack and get ready to leave. The relocation point was Ashkenazi Square. From there they would be evacuated through Zion Gate to the Israeli-held New City of Jerusalem.

The population of the quarter was now estimated at around twelve hundred. They had spent most of the siege huddled inside the Yochanan Ben Zakkai synagogue, whose four prayer halls were large enough to accommodate all noncombatants. This sixteenth-century synagogue had turned out to be an ideal twentieth-century shelter.

Dazed by the shelling, the civilians gathered up their belongings and trudged off to Ashkenazi Square. There I came upon a scene of human misery as old as time itself. Families gazed for the last time at their homes *(overleaf)*. It was past six and the setting sun cast a reddish glow on the ruined shell of Tiferet Israel—the Glory of Israel—which had served as a stronghold until the surrender. Now, with the top of its cupola blown off, the squat synagogue stood there like an amputated thumb. Night was about to fall on the last day Jews would pass in the Old City.

It was strange photographing a people who were being uprooted once again. Two thousand six hundred years ago, it had been the Babylonians who first drove the Jews out of Jerusalem. After them came the Romans, the Persians, the Crusaders. Now it was the Arabs. In some frightful way I had entered history when I marched into Jerusalem with the Arab Legion.

Shamelessly I stalked the dazed civilians while they assembled their belongings and trudged toward Ashkenazi Square. I was struck by their expressions, which had changed from a numb, empty look to one of grief. Yet no one wept. Tears were a luxury these people did not have time for. One hour was all they had to gather up the possessions of a lifetime.

I noticed how differently young and old reacted. Two young girls I photographed carried three bundles between them. They wore a look of determination as they strode forward. This was not true of the old Ashkenazi who sat cross-legged on the ground, removed from what was going on around him. All he had saved was a neatly folded prayer shawl and a thumb-worn holy book.

The woman with the infant in her arms just stood there. With unseeing eyes she gazed straight ahead, absorbed by some inner thought. The day before, her husband had been killed while standing by her side.

The old couple trudged up a hill leading to Ashkenazi Square. The woman held a cloth bag packed with food. She had also brought some matzohs in a paper bag. Her husband carried the family clothing. The two had just left the house they had lived in for over fifty years, never to return.

The old man, weighted down by bedding, staggered along with the frightened child toward Ashkenaz Square. There they got caught up in a human stream, which flowed past a young Arab irregular holding an automatic weapon. The refugees had no time for a last look at Rothschild House, pride of the quarter with its elegant archways and peach-colored limestone façade. The crunch of tramping feet over dusty rubble reminded me of a familiar sound I could not quite identify, until I closed my eyes. Then it came to me—it was like the surf rolling in along a pebbled beach.

In the uncertain light of dusk when colors fade to tones of grey, I photographed the refugees. Dr. Pablo de Azcarate, head of the United Nations Truce Commission, stood next to me.
"Misery always wears the same face," I said.
Dr. Azcarate nodded. "I'm a Spanish republican. It was just like this at Malaga during the civil war."

The first wave of refugees reached Zion Gate, border-line between Old and New Jerusalem. Once through the gate, the refugees would be in Israeli territory. Few looked back. One wistful boy did. A frightened girl screamed.

I walked back to the Street of the Jews. Arab civilians, in defiance of Major Tel's curfew, had come leaping over the rooftops like a swarm of locusts to loot. In their frenzied path fires sprang up. Black smoke billowed out of windows, while bright yellow flames licked wooden balconies. The entire quarter was now afire. The smell of burning mingled with the stench of death.

Distracted by the speed with which the Jewish Quarter was being destroyed, I almost missed the terrified little girl running down the street. In her terror she bared her teeth like a trapped animal.

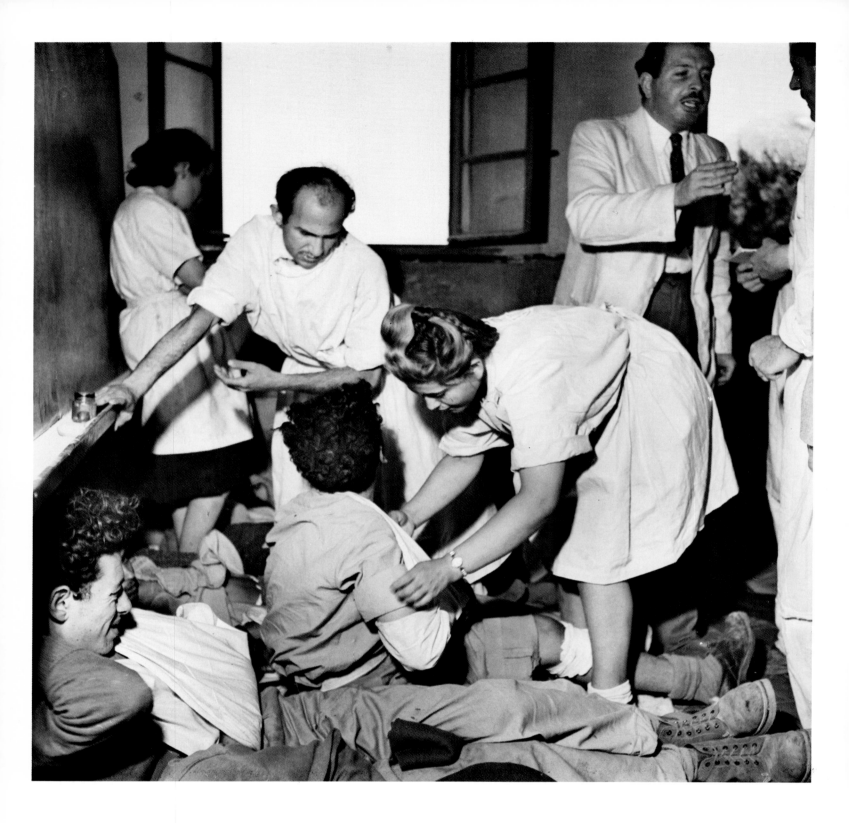

In accordance with the surrender terms, a medical board was made up of one Arab and one Israeli doctor, a representative of the Red Cross, and the United Nations representative. To this group the Mufti's nephew, Mousa el Husseini, had attached himself. His spotless white linen jacket and arrogant manner attracted a certain attention.

The ground floor of a building in Batei Mahse had been converted into a makeshift hospital. The minor casualties were being fed matzohs and jam. The nurse with blonde braids, a daughter of Mordechai Weingarten, was bandaging a lightly wounded patient. I estimated the wounded at more than two hundred and decided to photograph them after I had seen the refugees pass through Zion Gate. On my way out I came upon three corpses. Wrapped in sheets, they lay in the dim light of flickering candles. When I got back, the hospital was in flames. The wounded had been moved to the high-walled Armenian monastery, the safest place in the vicinity. Stretcher cases had been transported there by the Israeli medical team, assisted by Arab legionnaires. Only one fatality had occurred during the move. By decision of the medical board, the serious casualties were transferred to an Israeli hospital in the New City; the minor cases were sent to prison camp in Jordan.

Conditions in the hospital ward suggested the Crimean War rather than the twentieth century. The wounded lay on the same stretchers that had borne them in from outside. They still wore their dirty bloodstained uniforms. A few men rested on pallets so short their boots protruded from beneath the blankets. The flies were merciless, the heat intense, the stench unbearable.

In one corner a young boy, barely sixteen years old, lay back in his undershirt smoking a cigarette. His foot had been shattered by a burst of Bren gun fire. A round loaf of bread had been left on the mattress beside a wounded man who must have died soon afterward.

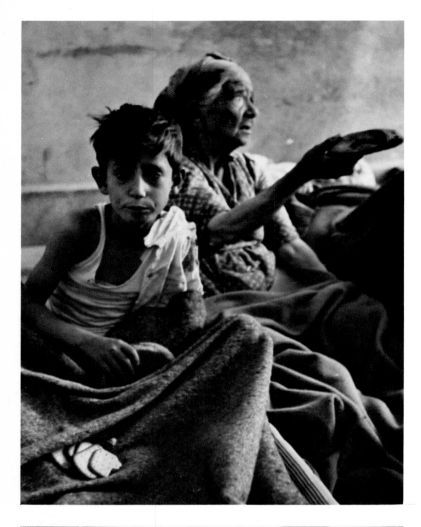

In a far corner of the ward a ten-year-old boy listlessly held a loaf of bread. His left shoulder had been shattered by a hand grenade. Uneaten biscuits littered the folds of his blanket. His expression was that of a wizened old man. I wondered if ever again he would be able to look at the world through the eyes of a child.

A young man lay unconscious from a head wound. He had strong, handsome features. He was clasping the hand of a nurse who covered her face in grief.

In the hallway a body lay on a stretcher covered with a sheet, the left foot projecting from beneath it. One of the doctors stopped by. "His name was Yitzhak Mizrachi," he said. "He could neither read nor write, but he was a real hero. War reveals men like that. To us he was the symbol of a simple man who fights for his people. When he was brought in yesterday morning word quickly spread that all was lost."

Outside, the Jewish Quarter burned like a pyre.

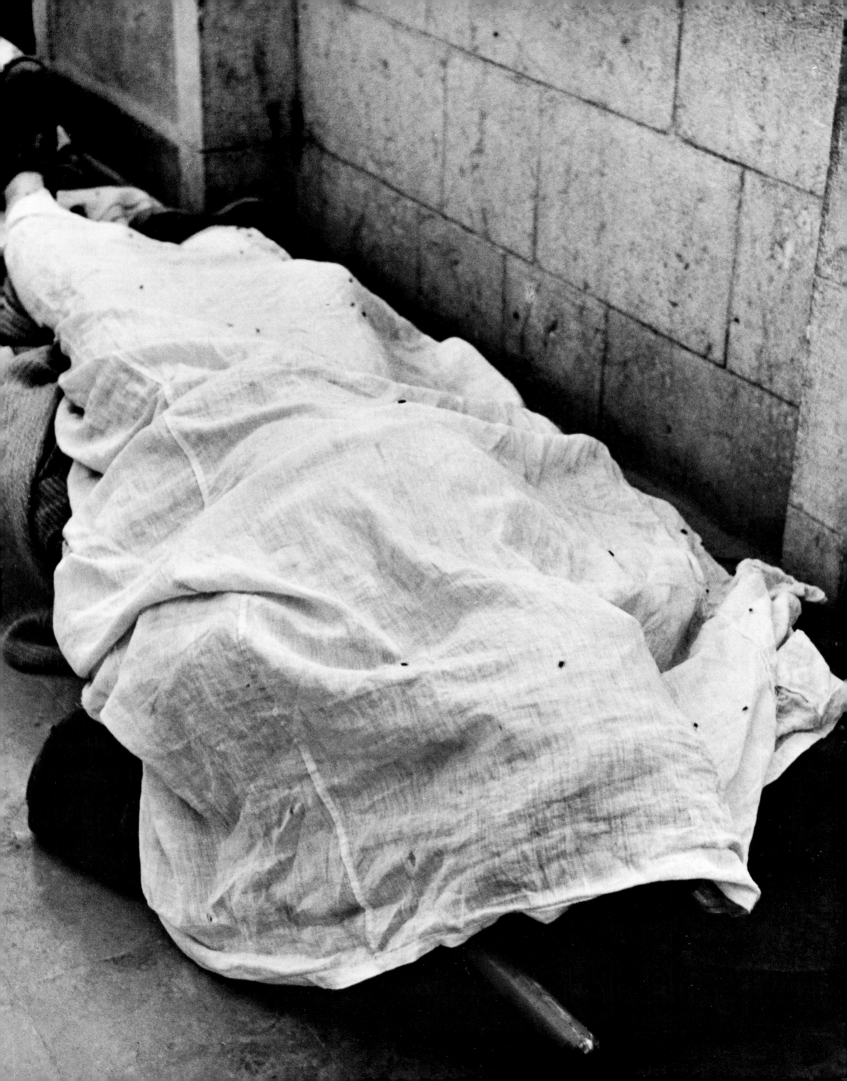

On May 29 the Jewish Quarter was a charred and burned out shell. Down Beit El a proud Moslem led the way, followed by his barefoot wife carrying three wooden containers of Sephardic scrolls from a nearby synagogue, and his daughter balancing a carton of matzohs on her head. Along Batei Mahse Street, which looks out on the Mount of Olives and the Russian church, Arab civilians were gathering up what little was left to plunder—nondescript pieces of shelves, window frames, boxes.

Near Sha'ar Hashamyin a more fortunate Arab had found an entire door he was carting off.

Batei Mahse, which only the day before could have
been the setting of a Sholem Aleichem story, lay
ransacked. Its former inhabitants were now refugees
in the New City of Jerusalem. Fighting would go on,
interrupted by uneasy truces and cease fires, until a
final armistice, signed with Syria fourteen months
later, brought the Israeli War of Independence officially to an end.
My last recollection of the Jewish Quarter on that
afternoon of May 29, 1948, was the sight of a charred
body in a doorway—the last Jew in the quarter for
nineteen years to come (overleaf).

The Search

For months after the surrender of the Old City I had a recurrent dream about the Jewish Quarter. I would re-enter Ashkenazi Square, where the Haganah prisoners were lined up. A frail youngster in an oversized Eisenhower jacket would cover his mouth in dismay when he saw me. Arabs were hauling mattresses out into the courtyard of Batei Mahse and ripping them open in search of gold. A child's feet in charred boots protruded from under a door placed over the body like a shroud. Before I could take a picture, Arabs were upon me. What made the nightmare so vivid was that it had all happened to me.

In time I got over these hellish dreams. But I never forgot the individuals emerging from the faceless crowd. Whenever I went over my old prints of the surrender I wondered what had happened to all these people, frozen in the postures I had once caught with my camera. What had become of Tawil, the Haganah officer who negotiated the surrender? What of Rusnak, the somber commander who signed it? Had the terrified little girl running down the street ever caught up with her family? Had the young boy with the vacant look ever recovered from the shock of his mangled shoulder? What were all those prisoners lined up in Ashkenazi Square doing now? What did they look like, a quarter of a century later?

No wonder I was curious about what had happened to those people, for I had photographed them at the very moment they ceased to exist as a community—an entire population uprooted and scattered. Whenever I went over the prints I would speculate as to their fate, aware I would never get an answer to all the questions that came to mind.

Then one day fate intervened.

Ted Rousseau, of New York's Metropolitan Museum of Art, was a friend of many years. The last time I saw him he told me he felt the Metropolitan ought to acquire some of my photographs. On hearing of his death in December 1973, I presented the museum with fifteen of my pictures in his memory. Thomas Hoving was especially struck by two of them: the neighborhood of Batei Mahse before and after the looting. Wanting to give the Metropolitan larger blow-ups than I could handle in my own darkroom, I took the work to my friend Ralph Baum, who presides over the Modernage Laboratories and specializes in exhibition prints.

In February 1975, Baum called me up to ask for the Batei Mahse pictures. He was going to Israel and wanted to show them to Teddy Kollek, the mayor of Jerusalem. Baum telephoned after his return to say that Teddy Kollek wanted to meet me on his forthcoming visit to New York.

I met the irrepressible mayor in May at an Italian restaurant, where I got my first glimpse of his working habits. While nibbling at a piece of Parmesan cheese and sipping a glass of Tio Pepé, he produced a dictating machine from his shirt pocket and noted that I had taken up his invitation to visit Israel, view

62

the restoration work in the Jewish Quarter, and seek out and photograph survivors of the 1948 siege for an exhibition at the Israel Museum in Jerusalem.

At first the idea of finding people uprooted from their homes three wars and a quarter of a century ago sounded preposterous. All I had to go on were old prints of people whose appearance would no longer match my pictures. My only hope was to find someone well acquainted with the Jewish Quarter who would recognize the individuals I had photographed in 1948 and could tell me of their present whereabouts—a tall order that Mayor Kollek promised to fulfill.

Teddy Kollek had Mrs. Rivca Weingarten in mind. She was a daughter of the late Mordechai Weingarten, whom I had photographed at the time of the surrender.

My wife Anna Maria and I landed in Israel on August 10, 1975—the first of three visits related to the work on this book. We stayed at Mishkenot Sha'ananim, Jerusalem's magnificent guest house for visiting artists. Mishkenot is located in Yemin Moshe, a section of Jerusalem which looks up at the old walled city. It was from Yemin Moshe that the party sent to relieve the Jewish Quarter on the night of May 18, 1948, set out. From the wide veranda of Mishkenot you can clearly follow the route the troops took up the rugged slopes leading to Mount Zion and the gate they would break through and enter.

Peter Halban, Mishkenot's director, was sympathetic to the problems surrounding our enterprise and helpful in every way. He found us two young Israeli students, Udi Sternbach and Alfredo Trapunsky, to act as assistants, guides and, on occasion, interpreters, in our search for the survivors.

Rivca Weingarten was the first person we visited. Her old family home in the Jewish Quarter is now a museum. Rivca began by telling us about her late father, Rabbi Mordechai Weingarten, a participant in the surrender.

"I lived with my father in the New City until his last day," Rivca recalled, "and witnessed the life he led after the fall of the Jewish Quarter. Well, he just couldn't recover. His heart was completely broken. He behaved as if his only child had died. He no longer attended any public functions, not even family ones. This man, who was once involved in everything that happened in Jerusalem, kept to himself. My children couldn't play the piano when he was present . . . we couldn't turn on the radio . . . we couldn't even laugh too heartily. The atmosphere in the house was very solemn and very, very sad."

Magnifying glass in hand, Rivca Weingarten pored over my pictures. She identified thirty people whom I had photographed in 1948. Eight had died. Of the twenty-two left, there were seven for whom we had no clues—no telephone numbers, no addresses, no names of friends or relatives. Eventually we found out that five had disappeared without a trace. The sixth never answered any of the forty-odd calls we

put through to him, nor did he reply to our letter after we finally managed to locate him. The seventh was a teacher Rivca had lost touch with years before, when the woman had moved to Beersheba. After a lot of detective work, Anna Maria finally traced her to Tel Aviv where she now teaches school and raises a family.

Rivca provided us with the addresses of the remaining fifteen and even phoned fourteen to alert them to our visit. (She did not call the fifteenth, with whom she is not on speaking terms.) Only one of the fifteen flatly refused to be photographed—on religious grounds. The others welcomed us with lavish arrays of pastry, coffee and fruit juice, though we frequently appeared at their homes early in the morning. And they obligingly submitted to interviews. Meeting these survivors was an emotional experience for all of us. Each of them reacted in much the same way. At first they looked over my pictures in stunned silence. It was as though they had just been taken prisoner again and were still dazed. Suddenly they would recognize old friends or relatives and this would trigger long forgotten memories, releasing a torrent of recollections as they relived the past. This did not necessarily mean they knew where to reach the ones they recognized, since they often had lost touch with one another. One survivor remarked, "Going to prison together doesn't necessarily create social contacts." But at least Anna Maria and her team had names to go on.

Having a man's name did not always reveal his true identity. On the day we arrived in Jerusalem we were greeted by Yissakhar Ben-Yaacov, a special assistant to Mayor Kollek. Yissakhar was called Jacobson before he took the name of Ben-Yaacov, which means "son of Jacob" in Hebrew.

Tawil, the young Haganah officer who negotiated the surrender of the Jewish Quarter with Major Tel, was another such case. We discovered he was now called Tuval. In accordance with a Foreign Office ruling, Tawil had taken the Hebrew name Tuval after entering Israel's diplomatic service.

Our "identity crisis" was compounded by the complexity of rendering Israeli names phonetically from Hebrew script into the Roman alphabet. There are no set rules or standardized ways of transcription. As a result the name Levy, for instance, can also be spelled Levi, Lewi, Lewy. We solved this problem by asking each person we interviewed how he wanted us to spell his name in the book. This is why Pinchas Oestreicher spells his name differently from Mordechai Pinkas.

We had a similar problem with street names. Batei Mahse is also spelled Baté Mahse, Battei-Mahssé, Battei Masche and Battei Mahasse, depending on what guidebook or map one is referring to. In such cases we took the spellings on street signs, which sometimes conflicted with the guidebooks.

The following excerpt from a tape made in Tel Aviv during an interview with Rivca's sister, Masha

Kaplan, will give an idea of how we conducted our search and located people. Masha, looking over my pictures, said:

	"This one I can recognize. His name is Alshek. He works as an orderly."
PHILLIPS:	"Where?"
MASHA:	"In Jerusalem."
PHILLIPS:	"Are you sure?"
MASHA:	"Yes, why?"
PHILLIPS:	"Because every time I've asked about him in Jerusalem, I've always got the same answer—'We don't know him.'"
MASHA:	"That's Alshek, all right. I'm sure of it. I knew him well."
PHILLIPS:	"How do you spell his name?"
MASHA:	"A-L-S-H-E-K. His first name, if I'm not mistaken, is Yehuda."
PHILLIPS:	"Where can we find him?"
MASHA:	"The last I heard he was an orderly at Hadassah hospital."

There we located Yehuda Alshek.

In the course of these interviews I was also able to clear up some impressions that had dogged me since 1948. My picture of the dead man with his face covered in the hospital ward has been considered one of the most tragic in my collection. For almost twenty-eight years I had felt that this picture of the round loaf of bread on the dead man's pillow was symbolic of life and death.

"He's not dead!" nurse Ora Dagan exclaimed when I visited her at Kibbutz Usha. "His face was split wide open, so I covered it to protect him from the flies." Ora was not positive about her patient's name. "I think it's Mishale," she said, "but I'm sure Dr. Riss (page 76) will remember. He operated on him."

Dr. Riss agreed that his last name was Mishale. "His jaw was shattered by a burst of Bren gun fire," he recalled. "He had swallowed his tongue and I pulled it out of his throat with forceps and without anesthesia." But Dr. Riss just could not remember Mishale's first name.

"Mishale's first name is Moshe," Yitzhak Ishai, a customs inspector told us a few days later. "He works at the post office here in Jerusalem." We got no further with Moshe Mishale until I photographed Yehuda Alshek.

"I know Moshe well," Alshek said. "He works for the municipality of Jerusalem." I had walked past Mishale's office every time I visited Mayor Kollek.

Wherever men gather, there is always one whom misfortune trails like a shadow. "Asher Zedira was such a man," Judge Moshe Hasson (page 150) reflected with a sigh when he spotted Zedira's gaunt features in my shot of the prisoners' line-up on Ashkenazi Square (page 31). Then he told me about his first meeting with Zedira on the day this unfortunate fellow joined the unit assigned to reinforce the Jewish Quarter. "I feel pity for all of you," Zedira told Hasson, "because you are going to be taken prisoner in the Old City. Why am I so sure? Because I am always taken prisoner."

Zedira proceeded to clarify his Delphic prophecy. He had first been interned by the Russians in 1939 when they occupied part of Poland. On his release Zedira left Russia and joined the Polish Corps shortly before it was sent to the Italian front, where not very long afterward he was taken prisoner by the Germans. Liberated on VE Day, he emigrated to Palestine and joined the Haganah. Sent into the Jewish Quarter, he and the other fighters were taken prisoner by the Arabs, just as he had forecast.

"Where can I find him?" I asked Moshe Hasson.

"You can't," he said. "Asher Zedira has taken his misfortune with him to Canada."

The one survivor who should have proved the most difficult to see turned out to be the most accessible—Mordechai Gazit, political advisor to the prime minister. The problem was not so much finding out who he was, but where he was. At the time, Gazit was shuttling between Jerusalem and Washington with Henry Kissinger, U.S. secretary of state, who was negotiating the Sinai Agreement. I never expected the message I got from Mayor Kollek advising me that Gazit would see me at the Foreign Office that same day. For over an hour Gazit recalled the part he played in the siege of the Old City. When I thanked him for granting me so much of his time, Mordechai Gazit said, "I'm in no hurry right now. I'm between jobs." Agreement on the Sinai had been reached.

Ironically the one survivor who lives closest to me was the one I had to travel the farthest to see. He was Leonard Binder (page 176). Binder was a young American visiting Palestine when the war of independence broke out in 1948. He had volunteered and fought in the Old City. After the war, he had returned home. Judge Hasson told me that Binder was now teaching political history in the United States, but the judge could not remember where. Back in New York I phoned Brandeis University since Binder was originally a Bostonian. He did not teach there. I called up Harvard and MIT without success. At a loss I communicated with Yaacov Levy, the Israeli consul in New York, and asked if he had any idea how I could locate a middle-aged Bostonian named Binder who had been to Palestine in his youth, fought in the Old City and was now a professor of political science somewhere in the States. The consul went to work on my request. According to some old files, a man who appeared to meet my description taught at the University of Chicago. I called Chicago on the off chance this might be the Binder I was seeking. The man I got on the line was indeed the right Binder. I flew out to Chicago to see him. He was the fifty-first, and last, survivor I was to interview for the book.

The people I have interviewed share one common denominator. They were all in the Old City during the last ten days of the siege. With the sole exception of Albert Melville, the British deserter, all were Jews. But among them were representatives of many countries. Their backgrounds and education varied greatly. Therefore it was natural that what these people recalled and the terms in which they related their experiences would vary. For some, certain events still stand out sharply twenty-eight years later. For others, these events might never have occurred. Yet each one's personal account interlaces with the rest. A chance remark by one confirms an important statement by another. Dr. Egon Riss recalls how Mousa el Husseini tried to stir the Arabs into a frenzy at the time of the surrender in the hope they would kill all Jews in the old quarter. A young girl remembers how the Arabs, suspecting the Israelis would take advantage of the cease fire to infiltrate their lines, started shooting wildly as the refugees passed through Zion Gate.

Everyone I talked to was extremely candid and open. With a single exception, all understated their experiences. The only exception was less a case of boastfulness than a flamboyant rendition of one man's achievements. "What d'you expect?" an Israeli friend remarked. "He's Hungarian."

There were discrepancies in what I was told. I have not attempted to correct them because I believe they add much to the veracity of the individual accounts. How could anybody expect these people to recall the number of weapons they had or how many fighters were involved? Under the circumstances, such discrepancies are normal enough. Records were never kept.* Mordechai Gazit, the commanding officer of the force sent in to relieve the Jewish Quarter and an extremely precise man, simply recalls having "ninety-seven or so men."

While each person interpreted the historic event through his own field of vision, their cumulative perceptions together offer a panoramic picture of what it was like to be in the Jewish Quarter during the siege. What struck me most while talking to these people, from the Chief Rabbi of Haifa to a Jerusalem housekeeper, was that none indulged in self-pity. To my knowledge, only one person cracked up on account of the siege. Most, not to say all, of these survivors have fared well. All of them, with one exception, are married and have children.

*Even the Israeli copy of the surrender is missing. After signing it, Rusnak turned the document over to Mordechai Weingarten in the belief the rabbi would deliver it to the Israeli authorities. But Weingarten was interned; the document was mislaid and has never been recovered.

In only one area do the survivors differ greatly, and that is in their recollections of people they knew twenty-eight years ago and have not seen for years. Take Albert Melville, the British deserter. My memory of Albert Melville was based on what he had told me at the time of the Old City's surrender. I recalled his fear that Peter, the British deserter on the Arab side, would kill him. I had tried to locate Albert after the prisoners had arrived in Jordan to see if he had got there safely. Melville, I was told, had never reached the POW camp. I concluded that Albert Melville's fear of Peter shooting him had unfortunately come true.

In the summer of 1975 Dr. Riss and I were going over my old photographs in Haifa when we came to Melville's picture (page 29). Dr. Riss remembered Albert clearly: "He showed up with his regulation rifle and, like a good British soldier, 250 rounds of ammunition and some hand grenades. He was a professional soldier. Our senior physician, Dr. Lauffer, who knew the British well—he had served with them as a medic during the Ethiopian campaign in World War II— tried to find out if Albert's appearance on the scene was not, perhaps, some kind of trick. The doctor spoke to Albert and studied his papers. 'Look,' he told me later on, 'anyone who's served for so long in the British army without getting any further than he has is either an idiot or a decent chap.' Albert turned out to be a decent chap and a very good fighter. I don't know why he ever joined us. Maybe it was out of idealism. He certainly didn't do it because we looked like the winning side."

"Why, there's Albert!" Judge Hasson exclaimed when he saw Melville's picture. "He came over to us with his rifle and two grenades and fought alongside us throughout the siege. When we were taken to prison that first night, an Englishman came up to him and said, 'Your side has lost. Why don't you join us now?' I remember Albert's answer: 'I'm going to stick with them wherever they go.' So he came to Trans-Jordan and was in prison camp with us."

"Are you sure of that?" I asked in surprise.

"Certainly," Hasson said. "Not only was he in prison camp, he returned with us to Israel. After that he joined the Israeli police force. Then one day, about eight years ago, he came to see me for legal advice, because he intended to go home. He was still considered a deserter by the British. I told him, 'Go back to England. Tell them your whole story and plead guilty. I don't think you will be severely punished.' Later I heard that he had been sentenced to eight months. Afterwards he visited his parents in England, then returned to Israel and married a Jewish girl. But it's been a long time since I last saw him."

"Albert was an idealist," Joseph Almog said as he studied Melville's picture. "He liked adventure and detested the Arabs. If I'm not mistaken the Arabs had once thrown him out of a cafe—right through a plate-glass window. I remember he was good at sports. He used to play soccer with us while we were in POW camp. After we got out of prison, Albert joined the army, then became a policeman. Later he married a local girl, left the police, and became a construction worker. The last time I saw Albert he told me he was going back to England, face charges, and serve three months in jail. He would then be reinstated as a British subject. Albert took his wife with him to England. That must have been ten years ago."

By then it was obvious to me that Albert Melville had reached Jordan and survived Peter's threats. Just how he had managed to do this did not become clear to me until I spoke to Moshe Rusnak, who had been in command of the Jewish Quarter. "Albert wasn't a Jew," Rusnak told me. "But we didn't want the Arab Legion to know who he really was, so we gave him a Jewish name. We called him Avraham Cohen. That's why you were told there was no Englishman among the prisoners."

The fifty-one people I interviewed form an extraordinary group. Had Hollywood ever decided to make a superproduction on the battle of the Jewish Quarter, I am sure the scenarists could not have dreamed up a more remarkable cast of characters than fate selected for me. When I expressed astonishment at the cross section of Israeli society I had photographed at random in the midst of a military debacle, Judge Moshe Hasson said to me, "In 1948 there were no more than 600,000 Jews in all of Palestine. We didn't even have a state of our own, and lived in a land controlled by Britain. These 600,000 Jews were surrounded by the armies of Egypt, Lebanon, Syria and Trans-Jordan. When the fighting started these 600,000 succeeded in defeating all the Arab states. You may well ask how we did it. We did it because we were an elite who believed in Zionism. Now that you have followed the trails of the people you met in Batei Mahse twenty-eight years ago, you will appreciate their achievements because, you see, our army was made up of civilian volunteers. If you had taken similar pictures of any other group of soldiers about to go into captivity and had followed their careers, I don't believe you would have found as many people who had made something of their lives. You now can get an idea of the type of soldiers we were at the time. Only one of us has remained in the army."
He is Colonel Mordechai Pinkas (page 170). Besides the colonel, the other fifty are:

66

On my return to New York from Jerusalem—where I had gone to gather additional material for the book, as well as attend the opening of my exhibition on September 21, 1976, at the Israel Museum—I found a letter waiting for me. Hevel S. Carmy had written to say that I missed seeing him in Israel during my quest for survivors.

In great detail Carmy described his dismay and disappointment that no one had brought him to my attention. "You will recognize me by my pointed woolen cap, my tunic with epaulets, my almond eyes and my aquiline nose, especially in one picture you took of me in profile where I am standing, head slightly bowed, among the prisoners," he wrote. From his description I immediately spied Carmy in my picture of Ashkenazi Square (page 31, picture 9). Carmy went on to say that he had written a personal account of the siege "because, in spite of the shock caused by our sudden captivity, I was so immersed in the impressions of those fateful days that I was determined . . . to put them down while they were still fresh in my mind and before time could erase them forever."

Carmy expressed regret that I had missed the opportunity to read his diary. But all that I could do in response to his plaint was to identify him in my picture of the prisoners, since my publishing date was now close at hand.

Early in December I received a letter from Martin Weyl, chief curator of the arts at the Israel Museum. Martin reported that "crowds and crowds" were coming to visit my exhibition at a rate of fifty thousand a month, among them Israel's chief of state, President Ephraim Katzir. President Katzir had recognized Rivca Weingarten, the first person I had met when starting my search for the survivors. I had come the full circle, the search was now over.

Next Year in Jerusalem

Standing where I had once crouched to shoot a picture of Porat Yosef under fire in the spring of 1948, I could not believe that I was in the same place. The only remaining landmark was the old wall and its battlements, which girdled the ancient city. Where the old nineteenth-century Porat Yosef compound had once stood, a huge crane now towered over the neighborhood, twentieth-century symbol of the Old City's reconstruction program.

The peach-colored limestone buildings shimmered in Jerusalem's crisp sunlight. The setting was vaguely familiar. It was as though I had stood here once before. This puzzled me, since the construction program had only been started a quarter of a century after I had last been here. Then I saw the street sign. It read: Batei Mahse (right).

Sha'ar Hashamyin looked familiar to me. The only change was the street's name. Once called The Gate of Heaven, it had been renamed Galeed. *Galeed* is the Hebrew word for "small wave." This is part of a trend to simplify street names (above).

I tried vainly to find a suitable angle to duplicate my
picture of the battered square, where I had photographed the civilians being rounded up in 1948
(above), to illustrate how radically the neighborhood
had changed. But I could not determine where the
old synagogue of Tiferet Israel would have stood
today in relation to the new buildings. I sought the
help of the city planners, whose offices are in Rothschild House (right). Even they were obliged to give
the matter some thought before deciding that, from
where we stood, the crane marked the old site of
Tiferet Israel.

Meir Alcotzer's features are timeless. He might have been one of the Israelites adorning the frieze on the Arch of Titus in Rome, or one of the Jews living under Ferdinand and Isabella in fifteenth-century Spain.

By Israeli standards, Meir has led a humdrum life. A descendant of Sephardic Jews expelled from Spain, his family came to Jerusalem via Yugoslavia. His mother had eighteen children. Only seven lived. Five were boys. Chaim (page 174) was wounded during the siege; Moshe joined a paratroop unit and was killed in 1954; Yitzhak and Yehuda are now in the army. Born in the Jewish Quarter, Meir lived there until he was taken prisoner in 1948. He was among the first to get back to the quarter after its liberation in 1967. "As a special favor a group of us who had fought in the Jewish Quarter were taken there in buses supplied by the municipality," he recalled. "The first thing I did was go to see my house. Nothing was left. Goats were kept in our demolished synagogues. It was no longer the Old City I knew. In my time the Jewish Quarter was one big family." By way of demonstration he looked at my pictures, ticked off the names of everyone he recognized, and in so doing helped calm my fears about finding people I hadn't seen in twenty-seven years.

For Meir Alcotzer the interval was no time at all. When I asked him where he had picked up his Spanish, Alcotzer said, "In Spain, five hundred years ago."

"In battle a soldier feels the elation of victory. For a physician war is entirely different," Dr. Egon Riss said as he flicked through his EKG charts with the precision of a metronome beat. "All I can remember of war is so many young people torn to pieces." Dr. Riss is Viennese like his childhood friend Teddy Kollek, the mayor of Jerusalem. Dr. Riss now heads the Department of Cardiology at Rambam Hospital in Haifa. I soon found out that he has many more views on war than his first disclaimer might suggest. Here are some of his recollections of the fighting in the Old City, where he served as a member of the medical team.

On entering the Jewish Quarter: "I remember the date exactly. It was April 28, 1948, seventeen days before the mandate ended. Dr. Peizer and I went in with the last convoy, relieving two other doctors on a rotation system. It was clear that the rotation business was over. When I said goodbye to the doctor I was replacing he said to me, 'See you after the victory.'
"It was equally clear that none of us would get out unless we won. So from the beginning it was a rather grim situation. No one thought he was doing anything unusual or heroic. It was just something that had to be done."

On the battle: "The atmosphere throughout the battle was a peculiar mixture of smoke, heat, the smell of the dead, and flies. But in the middle of a battle you are only aware of three things: the enemy, your buddies fighting alongside you, and the wounded. You don't have time for anything else. In battle I learned one impressive thing—the best soldier is not necessarily the best-trained man, not even the strongest, but the most decent, the one who does his job and takes care of his buddy. You don't need much education for that. You just have to be a reliable human being, and if you get into the terrible situation of a war it doesn't change you."

On the civilians during the battle: "The Arab artillery was what really disturbed the civilians. Their mortars were not very effective, however, because the houses of the Jewish Quarter had thick walls and deep cellars. Most of those who got injured and killed were civilians who panicked and ran out into the streets. It took a lot of effort to keep the civilians out of harm's way. If there had been fewer civilians we could have easily taken the entire Old City.
"I always slept wonderfully well when there was a bombardment. I knew that as long as they were blowing everything sky-high it was not at all serious. This was the so-called 'softening up.' It was a good time for everybody to get a rest. We just lay down and waited until it was over. When the artillery stopped and the machine guns opened up you still had time to get ready. But when the machine guns stopped you knew they were coming."

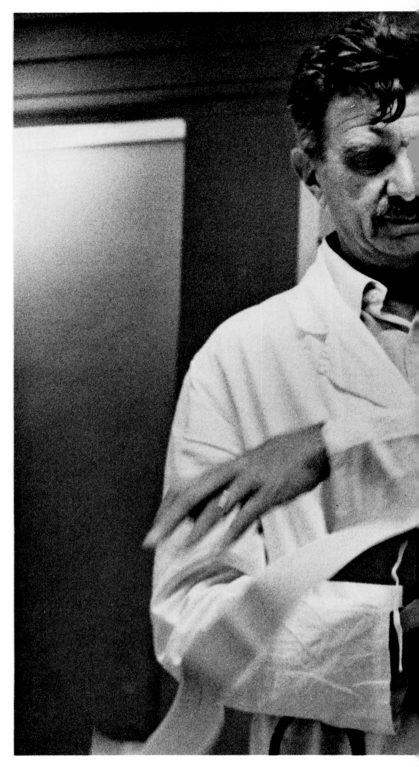

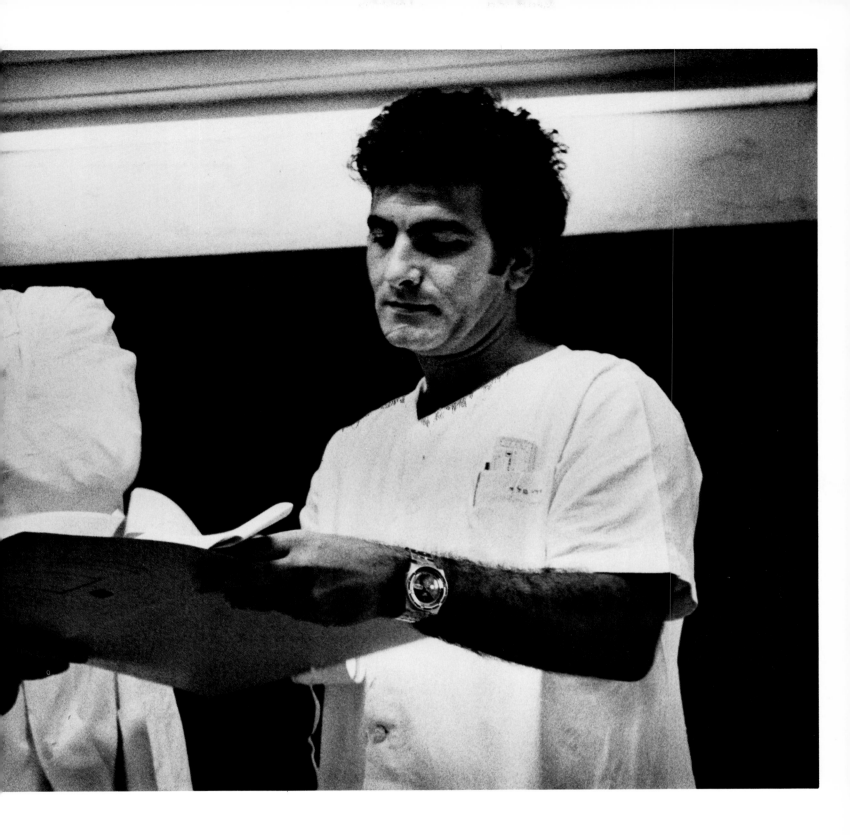

On the wounded: "The worst decision I had to make during the siege was what to do about the wounded after it became absolutely clear we could no longer hold the hospital in Misgav LaDakh. All of our wounded were there.

"My senior, Dr. Lauffer, said, 'I'm operating. You decide.'

"'Okay,' I said, 'we're moving tonight.'

"Moving to Batei Mahse was our only choice. That meant crossing a completely open area under a full moon.

"That night the Arabs fired off flares which lit up the open area we had to cross. They could have got every one of us with their machine guns. Fortunately they were very systematic and always fired their flares in the same direction, continually casting shadows in the same places. So I directed everyone to stay in the shadows while they crossed the area.

"I started by sending girls over to Batei Mahse to clean the rooms. Then I sent the first wounded out on mattresses carried by the more lightly wounded. After that we sent the operating equipment over. Then we moved those who needed surgery right away. Dr. Lauffer started operating in Batei Mahse that same night."

On the surrender: "There's one thing I'd like to tell you. Most people think that the Old City surrendered. Formally, yes. But the fact is, it fell. There were about thirty-four ... maybe thirty-five ... fighters still on their feet. They had no ammunition left. There were no white flags because there was no one to put them out.

"My participation in the war didn't end with the fall of the city. My war was the wounded. I went along with them to Jordan. We were in a military camp and, I must say, the Arab Legion's attitude was correct—in some instances really decent—towards the wounded. Remember that we had fought a very, very hard war against each other. Twenty-four hours earlier we could have killed one another without compunction, but after it was all over the legion behaved decently. I don't mean to say we fell about each other's necks in an embrace, but the relationship was correct.

"I was able to take care of the wounded prisoners. Major Tel honored his promise to return me with the wounded when they recovered. He was a soldier and a gentleman. Tel came to a tragic end, you know. He was accused of being involved in the murder of King Abdullah of Jordan—I say 'accused' because plotting an assassination doesn't go with his character. He was even condemned to death while in Egypt. But King Hussein, Abdullah's grandson, pardoned him five or six years ago. Tel returned to Jordan, where he recently died.

"Mousa el Husseini—the man in a white linen jacket who paraded around the hospital back in 1948 as though he were at a garden party—was a totally different type of man. He was a real Nazi. He was

married to a woman from Stuttgart and spoke German almost as fluently as I do. He had only a slight accent and must have lived in Germany for many years. When we were discussing what to do with the wounded, his approach was unlike that of the other Arabs. He was trying to get everybody killed. For instance, when the women and children were going through Zion Gate, he started the rumor that the Israelis were taking advantage of this to infiltrate the Arab positions. Such talk could have got everyone slaughtered. I went over to Major Tel and told him what was going on, and he put a stop to that nonsense. El Husseini was the main instigator in the murder of King Abdullah in 1951. He was later tried and hanged."

On the Jewish Quarter: "I had a dream which kept recurring over and over again through the years. It was always the same. I was somewhere in the Old City, wondering if we could have done things differently and saved the Jewish Quarter. All those who were in the siege told me they had much the same dream. Ever since the old quarter was liberated, the dream has gone ..."

On the Moslems: "The Arabs instinctively know the Jews consider Jerusalem spiritually theirs. They quite clearly recognize that, for Jews, Jerusalem is not houses or streets, but a spiritual attachment. Without Jerusalem there are no Jewish people. The Arabs are very much aware that giving the Jews such a foothold in Jerusalem is even more dangerous than giving them territory. It's that simple. The destruction of the Temple was the destruction of Jewish nationhood as such. The memory of the Temple, of the time before its destruction, along with the Talmud and the Torah, kept the Jewish people alive. For us, Jerusalem, the Wailing Wall, the remnants of the Temple, represent this sense of identity. As the Jewish religion is synonymous with the Jewish sense of identity, the two combined brought about a national group.

"There was a tolerant coexistence between the Moslems and the Jews in the Middle Ages. Although the Moslem religion was always established as the sole, dominant religion, their relatively benign attitude toward Jews was probably the result of their difficulties with the Christians.

"There's a lot of intolerance in the Moslem religion. Of course, I cannot say that the Christians were tolerant during the Middle Ages, and two thousand years ago the Jews were not tolerant either. But Jews and Christians have certainly changed, whereas the Moslems have changed little."

On the Palestinian Arabs: "Fifty years ago, if you had asked a Syrian, 'What is Palestine?' he would have said, 'Palestine doesn't exist. It's part of Syria.' If you had asked a Palestinian who he was he would not have said, 'I'm a Palestinian,' but, 'I'm an Arab.'

If you asked an Arab who had gone to high school, 'What is Trans-Jordan?' he would have said, 'It's a desertland east of the Jordan.' But he would never have thought of it as an Arab state.

"During the time King Abdullah had control of east Jerusalem he did nothing to establish his rule, or even his presence, there. He kept on living in Amman. Later his grandson, King Hussein, built a palace outside Jerusalem, but he never really left the Jordanian desert. On the other hand, if either Abdullah or Hussein had had the chance to occupy Damascus I'm sure they would have done so."

On Arab-Israeli relations: "I have no doubt that we can live together. There are three conditions in dealing with them: be strong, be independent, and respect them at the same time. The tragedy is that we are not communicating directly with them.

"I'll tell you a little story an Arab told me. Two blind beggars were sitting at Jaffa Gate, one on one side of the gate and one on the other. They were lifelong friends and divided whatever they had collected at the end of the day. One day a foreigner came along and said to one of the beggars, 'I have given your friend a shilling. Split it with him later.' Then he went to the other beggar and repeated the same thing. He gave neither one anything. As a result, these two lifelong friends became deadly enemies.

"Even if Israel had never existed, this part of the world would still be a place of terrible warfare among the various Arab states. As paradoxical as it sounds, I think what keeps the Middle East relatively peaceful is the presence of Israel. As long as Israel continues to be strong there will be peace. But if Israel didn't exist there is more than enough combustible material here to start a fire. The Arab argument that Israel is the disturbing factor is plain nonsense. The disturbing factor is their own disunity, their own rivalries.

"Our main problem is the difficulty in coming to terms with the Arabs, not because neither of us wants peace, but because the Arab who starts meaningful negotiations with us is attacked for it by all the other Arabs. The crucial fact is that a feudal situation exists among the Arabs. They don't think in terms of countries; they don't even think in terms of nations. They still think in terms of large family groups to whom they owe allegiance.

"This being the case, with whom is one to negotiate? With whom is one to come to a meaningful agreement? The man with whom you deal today is gone tomorrow. If the Arabs can't come to agreement among themselves, how can we come to agreement with them?

"I hope there will be peace in this region after the Arabs realize that Israel is here to stay, strong enough so that they can't overcome us on their own. When they slowly wake up to this fact, they may well say, 'Let's make the best of it and get together.'"

Uri Sigawi, assistant director of Jerusalem Customs, received me in his Jericho office. "I was born in Iraq, but I couldn't take it there," he said with a shrug. "I left Bagdad when I was sixteen, after a fellow at school kicked me and I let him have it back. Our teacher sent us both to the headmaster's office. He let the other boy go, and then he told me, 'Uri, as you're a Jew, you must keep quiet. You have to take it. Otherwise, you can't live here.'

"If the headmaster, who was a decent man, said I had to take it, then that was the way I'd have to live in Iraq. I went home and told my father, 'I can't stay here.' He couldn't read, but he could count. Father was a wealthy textile merchant who imported silks from India and Japan and could easily afford to pay for my education in Lebanon. I much preferred Beirut to Bagdad. I came to Palestine in 1944 and eventually the rest of my family followed me here."

Uri Sigawi was a member of the relief party sent into the Jewish Quarter during the siege of 1948. "My story is different from the others," he chuckled. "I was on leave from my unit. We didn't have water in our part of the New City, but there was a well near the home of my oldest brother. I called his wife and asked her to heat me some water so I could take a bath. I told her I'd be there at eight the next morning. When I got to her house with a fresh change of clothes the bath water was not yet hot. With nothing to do, I decided to go to my headquarters and see what was going on.

"When I got there I noticed a lot of fellows lined up. 'Today we have something on,' they told me. I joined them even though I hadn't been called up. We marched off, with me at the end of the line. At the depot gate they started to count off the men in front of me. 'You are number 101,' I was told, 'and we only have orders for 100.'

"'What do you care?' I said. 'One hundred . . . or 101 . . . it's all the same.' So they let me by.

"We were issued rifles and Sten guns. In the evening we moved up to Yemin Moshe, from there to Zion Gate and, after the breakthrough, into the Old City.

"Meanwhile, at my brother's house, they were wondering what had happened to me. Two or three days later my father went around to my headquarters and said, 'My son has disappeared.' They told him I was on an operation in the south and asked him to come back the next day. Whenever he returned they told him, 'Come back tomorrow.' This went on for weeks.

"Eventually my father got my first letter from prison camp. He took it to headquarters. Before he could say anything he was told, 'Come back tomorrow.' He showed them my letter. 'Mazel tov,' they said."

Uri Golani, a technical advisor to the United Nations, recalled his school days in Jerusalem over a drink at a Manhattan restaurant. "I was what you'd call today a dropout," he said. Golani is a hydrogeologist who specializes in finding underground water in underdeveloped countries. He gained experience in Israel, Nigeria and Iran and now travels extensively in Latin America. Golani is as casually sophisticated today as he was when, a very youthful-looking seventeen, he coolly operated a radio transmitter throughout the siege of the Jewish Quarter in Jerusalem. "The Haganah sent me into the Old City in November 1947," Golani said. "We had a secret radio station there. That's how I got stuck in the Jewish Quarter for six months before the war started. I don't know why I was selected as a radio operator trainee in the first place, since I had left school to become a locksmith. I don't think there was any special reason. "Our radio room was in Rusnak's headquarters. We received and broadcast messages and were in communication with the New City. Anyone could pick up our messages. We used a wireless, and didn't have any special frequency. Sometimes we used a code any child could decipher. We also had a telephone. From time to time I'd call my father. He lived in the New City and would try to find my voice on the radio. "On May 28 when the two rabbis first went to discuss the surrender, I reported it to the New City. It was a desperate situation and I was trying to keep the station working. There was no electricity so we had to operate with batteries. I had a small charger to keep them working. Finally I put in some olive oil, instead of engine oil, to keep the radio running. It worked. We went off the air about four o'clock. Later my father told me he kept trying to find me on the radio. He couldn't. There was only silence. He knew something had happened. After smashing the radio so it wouldn't fall into Arab hands, I went over to my quarters and packed a handbag and a rucksack. The first thing an Arab Legion guard did was grab them from me.

"My problem was that I didn't have shoes. I'd been working with some half-torn sneakers and remember worrying about this. One of the soles of my sneakers was open, and that really bothered me. 'You may have to march,' I kept saying to myself. Apart from that, I didn't have much reaction after we were taken prisoner. It had been a very tiring two weeks with almost no sleep. I can't remember what my feelings were at the time. I think there was no feeling. I was just numb.

"Once the battle was over, I didn't relive the whole scene afterwards. Rusnak (page 116) interviewed people again and again, trying to get a perspective. As far as I was concerned, it was over and done with. I never look back on the past. I don't even look forward. I just live in the present."

Nachman Burstein was born in Poland. His family emigrated to Palestine and moved into the Jewish Quarter when he was eighteen months old.

He was fourteen years old at the time the Old City surrendered. "He's such a little boy," his mother wailed as she and an Arab Legion officer tugged at Nachman, "you can't send him to prison!" Rabbi Weingarten persuaded the officer to allow the boy to remain with his mother. The legionnaire let the son go, but took the father instead.

Today Nachman Burstein owns a souvenir shop in Mea-Shearim, the orthodox neighborhood of Jerusalem. He belongs to a deeply religious group whose spiritual leader is Rabbi Nachman of Breslau, Burstein's namesake.

This nineteenth-century Hassid never permitted graven images of himself. As he once said, "If someone has a portrait done he adds a sin to himself and is no longer pure." So Nachman Burstein, whom I had photographed without his knowledge at the time of the surrender, amiably but firmly refused permission for me to take his picture when I called at his Jerusalem home twenty-eight years later.

At fifty, Avraham Weinfeld is still in the reserves. For thirty days a year he leads a two-man patrol along the very streets of the Jewish Quarter where he fought in 1948. In civilian life Weinfeld operates a construction company. But he was not always a builder. There was a time when he was a terrorist. Avraham Weinfeld was born in Millar, a Jewish district of Warsaw. His father made furniture, and employed fifteen workmen. In 1933 there was a bitter strike. A group of Jewish communists beat up Avraham's father because he was a capitalist.

"My father decided to emigrate to Palestine, where good carpenters were needed," Weinfeld said. "He came here with nothing but his two hands and made a fresh start in the furniture business. I was thirteen in 1939 when the British published their White Paper, which just about put an end to Jewish immigration. There were demonstrations against the British stand. On my way to school I saw the police beat up Jews who were protesting. This incident crystallized my political views. I joined the underground to fight the British.

"While I was with the Irgun, most of the other students belonged to the Haganah. The Haganah boys were a disciplined group. They did only what the Jewish Agency told them. The agency didn't want them to fight the British because they were at war with Germany. This led to internal clashes; you know what I mean—two Jews, three political opinions. Later on we all became one. But before that happened the British jailed me several times.

"The first time, I was taken to the *kishleh,* which explains why I later said, 'Back again!' when we were taken there after the Jewish Quarter surrendered in 1948. After two weeks I was paroled, on condition I stay at home between sunset and sunrise. I was arrested a second time when the police rounded up the usual suspects after an entire wing of the King David Hotel was blown up. I spent six weeks in jail. The third time it was a longer sentence. When I got out in the fall of 1947, fighting in the Jewish Quarter had begun. I was sent there because I had commando experience and knew how to make bombs."

Weinfeld was posted near the Hurva synagogue. It was from a window of this post that he observed an Arab irregular walking boldly up the street in his direction, arms laden with dynamite. "It was clear he planned to blow up our post," Weinfeld explained. "'What *chutzpah!*' I thought as I shot him."

Mrs. Masha Kaplan is the wife of Professor Isaac Kaplan, noted for his pioneer work in laser surgery. Her father was the late Rabbi Mordechai Weingarten, distinguished president of the Jewish community in the Old City of Jerusalem. Masha Kaplan is a remarkable woman in her own right.

Seated in the patio of her Tel Aviv villa, she recalled her family's close link with the Old City: "My family had lived there for over a century. We were all born and brought up in the same house. My mother's family came from Lithuania and my father's family from Galicia, which was then part of the Austro-Hungarian Empire. We lived in the Old City until 1948.

"The Arabs used to call my father a *mukhtar*—Arabic for 'mayor.' There's a difference between a *mukhtar* and what my father was. A *mukhtar* is appointed by the government and is salaried. Father was not an appointee and was never paid. He was the chosen president of the Jewish community.

"I was never a political person and to this day I don't belong to any political movement. You see, I'm a nurse by profession and when the trouble started I knew I would treat all—whether Jew or Arab or Christian—in the same way. Therefore I didn't join any group. You must also remember that I came from an orthodox home. We were brought up to be very broadminded, both politically and religiously. We never differentiated among people.

"My father ran a polyclinic for the inhabitants of the Old City. Jews, Christians and Arabs got free medical aid. I was the nurse in charge. Throughout the siege we continued giving treatment to all the inhabitants. I wasn't a qualified midwife, but I delivered infants, several from Arab women."

In the hope that Masha could help me identify the wounded fighters, I showed her my pictures of the hospital ward.

"My God, it's been such a long time since I've seen these people . . . such a long time!" she exclaimed. "I know every single one of them. I would recognize them on the street. But the thing is, as a nurse I have been continually involved with lots and lots of people in my profession. In 1949 I helped take care of fifty thousand Yemenites. Then I accompanied my husband to Vietnam, where he set up a hospital. For the past three years now I have been traveling with him almost every other month, whenever he attends a medical convention or delivers a lecture, always meeting new people. Even so, I do recognize these people from the old quarter. I know who they are. Every one of them. I can even recall their wounds. But I simply can't remember their names.

"You know, the siege began on the twenty-ninth of November, 1947, with the announcement of Partition. It ran from November 29 to May 28. When the real fighting started we divided the Old City into separate parts in case one section fell. I was put in charge of the upper part. I took a wing of our house and turned it into a hospital.

"We had three hospitals in operation. The first to fall was our house, then the polyclinic, and finally the regular hospital itself. That was when everybody was moved to Batei Mahse. We were only three nurses—one was a theater nurse who was in the operating room with the doctors; one was a social nurse who looked after the inhabitants; I was in charge of the hospital.

"We had three doctors—Dr. Lauffer, Dr. Riss and Dr. Peizer. We operated under fire, using kerosene lamps. We had no antibiotics, no blood plasma. After operating the doctors had very little time for the patients, but they used to make the rounds of the wards. It was terrible to see all those young boys suffering. When I think how medicine has advanced since then, I realize how fortunate even the unlucky ones are today. We had absolutely nothing to treat our boys with, especially in the last few days.

"On May 15 every available person went to fight or look after the wounded. There was really no time to look after the dead. We simply piled them up in a mortuary. After nine days the stench was so terrible it was decided to bury the dead during a lull in the shelling. First they had to be identified. Unfortunately there weren't many volunteers. I was asked to go because I knew all the inhabitants of the old quarter and could also recognize the young soldiers from outside the Old City, having nursed them when they were brought into the hospital. My sister Judith (page 108) volunteered to come along with me.

"The two of us went to the mortuary. The bodies were already decomposing. When I tried to remove a ring from the finger of a young woman at the request of her husband who simply couldn't do it himself, the finger came off in my hand.

"The smell in the room was terrible. We had to put on masks before we started identifying the bodies. We wrapped them in sheets and put scraps of paper bearing their names on each and every one of them. My father had said we should at least do them a last honor.

"I also looked after a group of very old women I had been caring for since childhood. They lived on the border of the Arab Quarter. I went to see them every day, but once the shelling started they were removed to the synagogue with the rest of the inhabitants. When the civilians left the synagogue after the surrender I noticed that the old women were missing.

"By then the Old City was empty. I went back on my own to look for these women I'd grown so fond of. I found myself in an alley and, just as I was rounding the corner, saw a mob of Arab looters. The scene resembled what you'd imagine a pogrom would look like—people running away with eiderdown pillows and carrying off chickens. By the time I saw them I couldn't run back because I was already surrounded. I realized I would never get out alive.

"Fortunately, an Arab legionnaire saw somebody grab my hand to take my wristwatch. He fired into the crowd and told me to run for my life. I never did find out what happened to my old ladies.

"During the siege we took care of over two hundred wounded. That was quite a lot of work, considering there were only three nurses and three doctors. The seriously wounded didn't stand a chance. As for the others, it was a question of luck.

"After we surrendered, a team from the Red Cross and the United Nations decided who would be held prisoner and who would be released. Through error some lightly wounded went free; others who were seriously injured went to POW camp in Jordan. There were nine among those sent to the camp who were really seriously ill, who definitely needed many operations and a lot of treatment. One had such a serious head injury we didn't even worry about giving details on him. When the team came along he sat up for a few moments and gave his name. On the way to Jordan he suddenly went wild. He's never recovered.

"I went with the wounded to Jordan because there was no one to look after them. I wasn't in touch with my family and didn't know they were held hostage. It was only when I left with the stretcher bearers that I saw them being taken away to Amman.

"I only spent a few weeks in Jordan because my patients got better, and I realized that I could be more useful in Israel. When my family was repatriated I joined them and we came back together. I felt that a period of my life was over with. What upset me most was not just losing our house, it was losing generations and generations of history, so to speak. It wasn't a feeling of frustration. It was a feeling of heartache.

"I went to work in the surgery department at Hadassah hospital after I came back. Later a rehabilitation center for seriously wounded soldiers was opened, and I worked there until 1949. Then I was asked by the government to go to Aden and join Operation Magic Carpet. Magic Carpet was set up to handle the emigration of Yemenite Jews to Israel. These people had to make their own way to Aden, because the Arabs didn't allow us into Yemen. From Aden we flew them to Israel in chartered planes.

"When I was approached to do this work I didn't know where I was going. It was all very hush-hush because our planes were flying over Arab territory. Magic Carpet remained a well-kept secret until an American journalist happened to hear about the operation. She let the story out.

"The refugee camp in Aden was originally set up to handle two hundred. By the time I arrived, fourteen thousand Yemenites were already there, most suffering from tropical sores and eye diseases. During the year I spent in Aden we managed to airlift fifty thousand Yemenites to Israel. It was one of the most exciting years of my life.

"Back in Jerusalem, I worked in the children's ward at Hadassah. In 1954 I was sent to England to conduct a study on premature babies, because we

90

wanted to open up a premie unit. I came back and worked with our premie unit for a few years.

"I married Professor Kaplan in 1956. He opened the biggest plastic surgery ward in the country at Beilinson Hospital here in Tel Aviv. My husband was the first person in the world to operate with a laser beam clinically. You may have heard about it. Before that, the laser had only been used on animals. He's done over four hundred operations. The first one was performed here in Israel. My husband uses a special machine, the Sharplan 791, which he developed here in Israel with Uzi Sharon. This machine enables a surgeon to operate with very little bleeding. It is used on parts of the body where there is normally a lot of bleeding, or on hemophiliacs, because it seals up the blood vessels. There is hope that in cancer operations it will minimize the chances of malignant cells spreading throughout the body. This is really a major breakthrough in medicine.

"After my daughter was born I decided to make up my mind about what I wanted to do most. I realized that being a nurse, as I saw it, and being a good wife and mother just didn't go together. So I gave up my profession and became a housewife. Now I only do volunteer nursing in wartime.

"During the Sinai War I was in charge of the children's ward at Hadassah. We thought Jerusalem would be attacked, you know. Fortunately, nothing happened. In the Six Day War and the Yom Kippur War I worked in my husband's burns unit at Beilinson. Although I've volunteered to work with the burned soldiers in every war, I simply cannot get over the smell of burned flesh. It goes back to the siege. I was with a friend whom I don't want to risk identifying because her family is still unaware of what happened. A shell burst and killed her, while I came out scot-free. Her body was put in what had once been the free kitchen my mother ran for the poor. The body was burned to ashes after the Jewish Quarter was set afire. Now, whenever I smell burned flesh, or meat, I find it unbearable . . ."

I recognized Joseph Atieh, who teaches economics at the Hebrew University of Jerusalem, even though it had been twenty-eight years since I last saw him. He had caught my eye in 1948, as he stood in line with the other prisoners, because of a slightly comical bandage on the bridge of his nose. Now, as we strolled along the campus past a sculpture by Henry Moore, I noticed a gentleness in his tone when he spoke about the siege.

"I was an elementary school teacher when the war broke out," Attieh said, "and was put in the reserve. You see, we teachers were not recruited at first because there was the problem of keeping the schools going. We taught in the morning and at night were on guard duty. Of course the Palmach took a teacher if he was a good fighter, but if he was a good teacher and not a very great fighter they put him in the reserve. I was in the reserve. I was assigned to one of the groups on the north side of Jerusalem. The day before the breakthrough they took whoever was around at the time—ten from here and ten from there. As our group was in reserve, it was just an accident that I got sent to the Old City.

"As you may know, we went back home to eat whenever they didn't have food at headquarters. I lived only seven minutes away and had got back to headquarters from lunch just in time to hear them call out, 'Everybody here gets in the cars. We're going into the Old City.' If I had returned five minutes later I'd never have gone to the Jewish Quarter. It was fate.

"Our group was made up of forty young people and forty middle-aged men. We expected to support the breakthrough and had no idea we'd wind up defending the Jewish Quarter. During the first days we hoped that, as the Palmach had once succeeded in breaking into the Old City, they might do it a second time. Every night they said, 'Tonight we will break through. Tonight we'll do it.' But it never happened.

"Then on the morning of the twenty-eighth it was really bad. It was clear we couldn't hold out. They closed in on us slowly, you see, conquering one post after another. We were out of ammunition. I had about thirty rounds left. That's all. There was a feeling of uncertainty about what was going to happen.

"The most shocking moment came at around eleven in the morning. All the children and old people were in the synagogue when the Arabs got into the courtyard. The people all began crying out, 'Shema Israel!' —the prayer you repeat when you think it is the end, which goes, 'Hear, oh Israel, the Lord our God, the Lord is One!' There were twelve hundred people crying, 'Shema Israel!' You could hear it all over the Old City. It was awesome.

"We felt it was all over. It seemed to be a question of their killing us or taking us away. We didn't know. The UN people came. They said, 'It's all over.' What that meant, we still didn't know."

Israel Afri, one of the original members of the Jewish Quarter's defense unit, is a pastry cook. As a child he was smitten by the cheerful aroma of baking cake. In the early thirties few families in the Jewish Quarter had ovens in their homes, so Afri's mother would mix batter and send him to the bakery shop to have it baked for a small fee. He can still recall the long queues at the bakery before the holidays. He would wait his turn, balancing in both hands a doughnut cake with jam for Chanukah, a triangular pastry with poppy seeds for Purim, or a honey cake for Rosh Hashana.

Afri never outgrew his childhood infatuation for pastry. For the past twenty-three years he has baked a wide variety of cakes—including Mrs. Golda Meir's favorite type of strudl—at Nada, Jerusalem's popular pastry shop.

Few countries have such demanding pastry connoisseurs as Israel, where eating cake between meals is something of a cult. The day is first highlighted by the morning coffee break, featuring warm flaky croissants and cinnamon buns, and then by another one in the afternoon, when a richer, creamier variety of pastries is enjoyed.

"There is a big difference between an Ashkenazi's and a Sephardic's taste in pastry," Afri told me. "Take the wedding cake. European Jews like white ones with delicate flowers. An Oriental wedding cake is decorated in vivid colors—red, green or yellow. Europeans are interested in substance, Orientals in color."

An authority like Afri can readily tell a man's national origin by the sweets he eats. Austrians are partial to *sacher torte*, Hungarians to *dobos*, Russians to *torte Russi*, Poles to cheesecake, Germans to strudl. This is probably why the official who made up the menu for a dinner given by the Israeli Parliament in honor of Henry Kissinger selected strudl for dessert. Nada got the order, of course, and Israel Afri baked the three-foot cake.

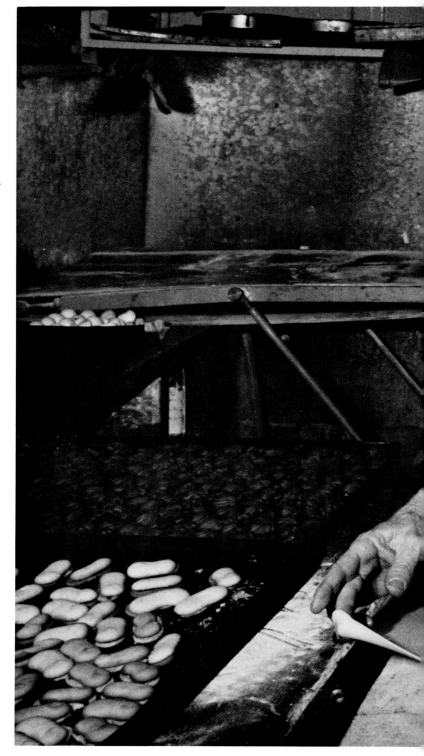

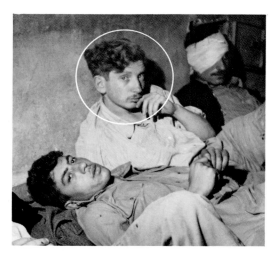

Yehuda Alshek works at the Hadassah hospital in Jerusalem. He applies plaster casts to fractured limbs in the orthopedic ward. His hobby is collecting the used and discarded casts that were decorated while worn by his patients and now constitute what some regard as the finest pop-art collection in Israel. Alshek was born in the Old City on the Street of the Jews, where his father owned a cafe. As a youth he studied nursing at a school outside the city walls. For this reason the British allowed him to move freely in and out of the Jewish Quarter at a time when they were guarding against the infiltration of Haganah fighters into the Old City.

After the fighting began Alshek worked as a hospital orderly. He got to know all the wounded and actually saved the life of Moshe Mishale (page 172), who had been left for dead in the morgue. Throughout the years he has kept in touch with a number of survivors of the 1948 war. Nowadays they occasionally drop in on him for medical advice on minor matters. "Only the other day one of them came to see me about his hemorrhoids," Alshek sighed. "We're all getting on in years."

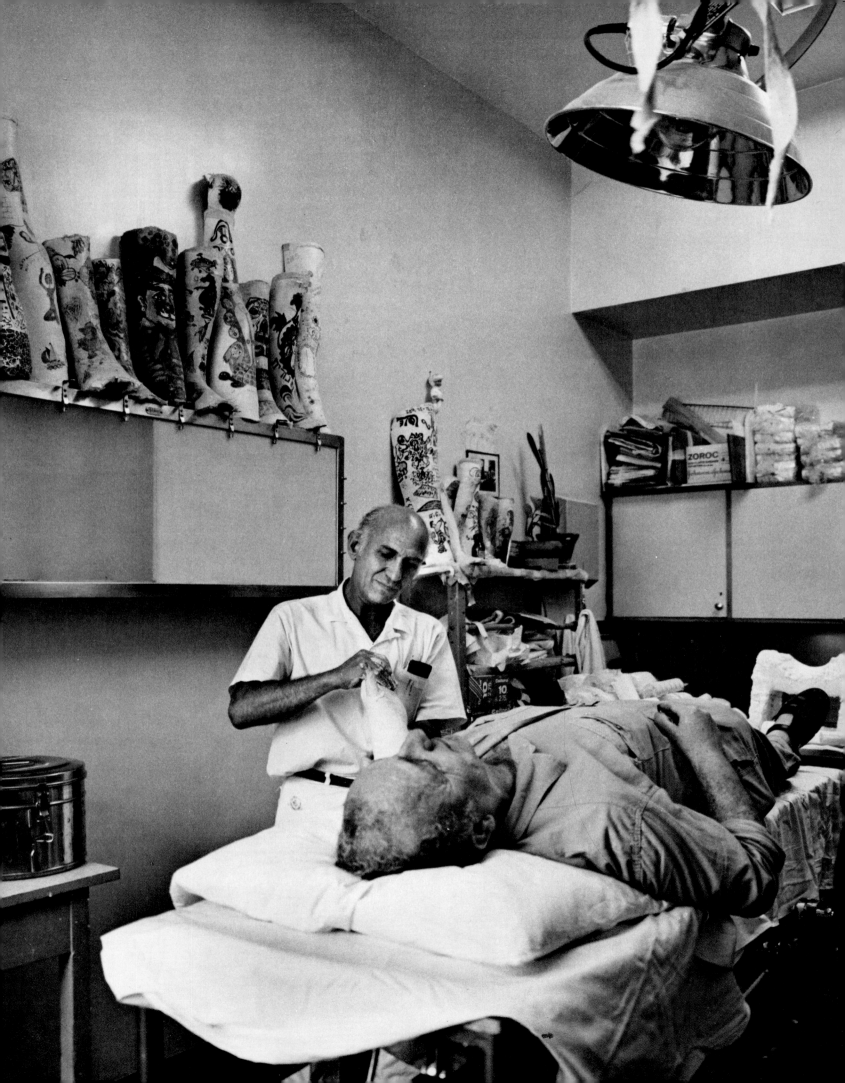

Shoshana Avidan was born in the Old City and lived on the Street of the Jews with her father (page 126), mother, brothers and sisters. "During the siege my older brother Shimon was killed one street away from the Hurva synagogue, and my older sister Shulamit was shot dead by an Arab sniper on Batei Mahse," Shoshana told me as she clutched the hand of her eight-year-old son Nir. They were looking at all that now remains of the Hurva. For Shoshana, such pilgrimages to the Jewish Quarter evoke many early memories.

At fifteen years of age Shoshana was a member of the Gadna, the paramilitary youth organization. Her superior officer was Chaim Avidan, whom she married in 1952. At first Shoshana ran messages, but soon she picked up an Enfield rifle from a wounded Haganah fighter and took his place at the barricades. On the afternoon of the surrender she dropped her rifle into a well to prevent its capture by the Arab Legion. Another girl was about to get rid of her revolver the same way when Shoshana took it and hid it in her bra. She then went to look for her mother at the Yochanan Ben Zakkai synagogue, which the civilians had been using as a shelter. Her mother was not there. Shoshana searched through the Jewish Quarter and finally spied her on Ashkenazi Square, where the civilians were being separated from the fighters for evacuation to the New City. She and her mother were then joined by her father, Shlomo Kubi, and her fifteen-year-old brother Rami. En route to Zion Gate, mother and daughter became outdistanced by father and son. Kubi and Rami were already through the gate, with Shoshana and her mother only yards away, when shooting broke out on both sides of the wall. The Arabs, fearing the Israeli fighters would take advantage of the dark to infiltrate the Old City, closed down the gate, and ordered the civilians to remain where they were.

Shoshana and her mother huddled together, the mother worrying that the Arabs would molest her attractive daughter, the daughter worrying that the Arabs would discover her concealed revolver. At her mother's suggestion, Shoshana put her overcoat on inside out and pretended to be retarded. She drooled at the mouth so convincingly that an Arab patted her on the back and said, "You poor child."

"Finally morning came," Shoshana recalled. "We were ordered to stand in line. Someone came toward us with a gun. We were really afraid they were going to finish us off. Then someone said, 'No, let them go.' So we went through Zion Gate. It was Saturday morning."

Israel Philipp is, in his own words, "a nice typical *yeki*." Reminiscing at the World Zionist Organization in Jerusalem where he is deputy director of archives, Philipp explained, "A *yeki* comes from *jacke*, which means 'jacket' in German and dates back to the days of the British mandate when German Jews dressed more formally than others here."

Philipp's life is the story of a bookish man who survived. Born in Breslau in 1915 when it was still a German city, he was arrested in 1938 during the anti-Jewish riots known as *Kristallnacht*—Crystal Night. Across Germany and Austria 7,500 Jewish shop windows were smashed and 191 synagogues destroyed. Philipp was one of 300,000 Jews arrested in retaliation for the murder of the third secretary of the German embassy in Paris by a crazed Jewish youth. "I only got out of concentration camp because I planned to leave Germany," Philipp told me. "While waiting for my Palestinian visa I had to report to the Gestapo every week to show them my passport and travel documents. In March 1939, I decided it was safer to leave for England, as my visa to Palestine was being held up. My father and the rest of the family stayed behind. Most of them were killed by the Nazis.

"I got to Palestine in 1940. In 1941 I joined the British army and served for five years. I was never especially good at physical activities. But I can still remember the time I was stationed at Porat Yosef during the siege of the Old City. I performed a real feat. The staircase of the building I was in had been shot away. To get out I had to make an awfully big leap to safety. If I hadn't made it, I wouldn't be here talking to you today."

Mrs. Simcha Mirski lives in Jerusalem with her son Abraham at 24 Haportzim Street. Mrs. Mirski suffers from chronic lack of memory induced by fear. When shown a picture I had taken of her with a small child in her arms at the time of the surrender, she insisted she did not know who the girl was. Eventually her son revealed that the child was her granddaughter Simka.

"Mrs. Mirski," I asked through an interpreter, "you say you don't know where your granddaughter lives. Would you know her married name?"

The answer was, "No, I don't."

"My mother," her son Abraham explained, "lives in fear. She can't forget the troubles of 1929, 1936 and 1939, World War II, or our war for independence. She remembers those were the years that great numbers of Jews were slaughtered. She can't forget that her husband was killed at her side during the siege of Jerusalem. Now she listens to all the news broadcasts on the radio and keeps asking me if there will be another war. She never goes to sleep without listening to the late news bulletins. Once I took her radio away from her. She went right out and bought another. 'The way you worry about war,' I said to her, 'you'd think you were Golda Meir.'"

Moreno Mizrachi sat at the drawing board in his Tel Aviv studio. A graduate of Technion, the Israel institute of technology, Mizrachi is a successful interior designer.

Moreno attributes his success to his wife Sophia, who was born in Bulgaria and emigrated to Israel in 1949.

Moreno was born in the Jewish Quarter. His family had lived near the Street of the Jews for five generations.

Moreno grew up in the Old City and belonged to the embryonic nucleus of the city's defense, which had been well prepared by Abraham Halperin. "By the time Partition was announced," Moreno said, "we were ready for any trouble. Halperin had organized the Jewish Quarter like Stalingrad. He had prepared us morally as well as physically. We had made tunnels leading from one house to another so we could fight without having to go outside. We wanted to be able to attack the enemy without him seeing us. We were divided into groups. Everyone knew his post. There were also reserve groups.

"This preparation would have been all to the good had Abraham Halperin been allowed to remain here. But the British expelled him from the Old City. Our plans got all mixed up. We fought as best we could for eighteen days and nights.

"When we surrendered I went to see my mother, who was paralyzed, to say *shalom* before leaving for prison camp. I thought she would be safe with my father. I had no idea that the Arab Legion would take him prisoner later on at Batei Mahse. On hearing the news my mother dropped dead on the spot.

"I only heard about it four months afterward. We have a tradition that, when someone in the family dies, you must sit for seven days. But if you hear about it months after, as I did, you only sit for one hour. I sat for an hour and, as a sign of mourning, cut a piece from my coat.

"After I met Sophia and we got married," Moreno explained as we sat in his modern studio, "she made me realize that I was a skilled carpenter with a gift for drawing. I would never make enough money to bring up a family the way we wanted, if I didn't start my own business. She was sure I could earn more, so I went to night school to study interior design. I was a carpenter from 7:00 A.M. to four in the afternoon. Then I'd come home, eat something, change my clothes, and go to school from six to nine. I'd do my homework until midnight. Every day for three years I did this. For the next seven I was employed by a large company until I was sure I could succeed on my own.

"From the day I married Sophia something in me changed. The traditions of the Bulgarian Jews are completely different from those we knew in the Old City. I became more and more like a European. Up to then my mentality had been more Oriental. I'm not even sure that I could live in the Old City now."

104

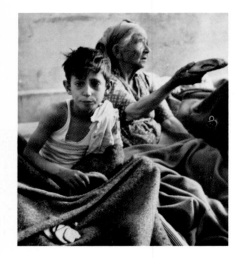

Refael Hanoch was ten years old when I photographed him in the Armenian monastery's makeshift hospital the day after the surrender. On May 26 he had been severely wounded in the left shoulder by a Mills grenade while posted as a lookout.

Hunger had driven Refael Hanoch to join the battle for the Old City. One night he crept out of the Yochanan Ben Zakkai synagogue, which had been turned into a shelter for civilians as the shelling grew in intensity. He reported to Shaul Tuval (page 112), in charge of the youth brigade. Tuval told him he was too young to fight. So Refael went to another unit, this one posted in a bakery shop. Enlisting there as a lookout, he found the rations plentiful.

"I ate well," he recalled as he told me how he had been posted at a small window which overlooked the rooftops. "My duty was to report at once any legionnaires I saw crawling over the roofs to attack us. I understand now why they made me a lookout. If I had been a grown man sitting at that window the legionnaires would have shot me on sight. Since I was a little boy, they didn't. But they must have grown suspicious of me, because they were taking losses. A legionnaire tossed a grenade at me."

According to Jerusalemites today, Refael Hanoch is one of the most sought after men in town—he is in charge of the telephone repair service.

Mrs. Judith Kammar, one of the Weingarten daughters, now lives in Tel Aviv with her husband, an ex-assistant attorney general. She recalled what life was like when she lived in the house on Or Hahaim Street in the Jewish Quarter of Jerusalem's Old City.

For five generations the house on Or Hahaim had been the home of the Weingarten family. The fate of this family and that of the Old City were bound together. Bombs were thrown at the house during the riots that lasted from 1921 to 1939. During the 1948 siege, one of the first shells to be fired hit the house on Or Hahaim. The shock left Rabbi Weingarten's wife paralyzed. By the time the Old City was liberated in 1967, Mrs. Weingarten had recovered. But on the day she was to return to her old home, she suffered another stroke. Although she lived for another five years, she never got back to the house on Or Hahaim Street.

"Before the First World War all the Jews were concentrated in the Old City," Judith Kammar related. "We had 25,000 people there. In one room you'd find a family of twelve. Our home on Or Hahaim was a big house, so we had only three girls in one room. My father, who became president of the Jewish community, took over the affairs of the Old City in 1921. He took charge of all the Old City's problems. He tried to keep people there and find work for them. The majority were very poor. We operated a free clinic and a free kitchen in which hundreds were fed every day. My younger sister Masha worked at the clinic. For many years I was my father's secretary.

"There was never any peace in the Old City. Fighting was a way of life ever since I can remember. Whenever there was trouble in the world the Jewish Quarter seemed to be the focus. The 1936 riots marked the beginning of the exodus from the Old City. Who wants to live in a place where you're always being attacked?

"Living there was very difficult for us as young girls. For instance, we had to go to school on St. Paul's Road in the New City. One day we were called from class and told to go home at once. There was a taxi waiting to take us to Jaffa Gate. A curfew had been announced. When I was older and going out with my future husband, I could only let him take me so far from home and bring me back again. If he brought me home after dark, the Britishers would detain him. He'd have to call my father, who would then go to the police station and get him released. We missed a lot of things other girls our age could do. Maybe our upbringing was more conservative than nowadays. Maybe we were less emancipated. But I wouldn't give up all those experiences for anything in the world.

"I went back to the old Jewish Quarter after the Six Day War. It was like going back to a cemetery and digging up a grave, wanting to see the beloved as he looked when you put him to rest. But what do you find? A bundle of bones."

Death and taxes being inevitable, I found both in Jerusalem. I encountered death in the Jewish Quarter in 1948 at the moment its thirty-five weary defenders surrended to the Arab Legion. Twenty-seven years later I came across the tax collector, while trying to locate these survivors. The twenty-third of the twenty-five fighters I managed to seek out was Shimon Levy. Mr. Levy today is a *mevaker mas hakhnassa*—in English, an internal revenue inspector.

Shaul Tuval was waiting for me at his desk in the Middle East section of the Foreign Office. I was lucky to find him still in Jerusalem. Tuval had been appointed Israeli consul in Istanbul, and within days was to leave for Turkey. He had been in Israel's Foreign Service since 1952, stationed in Ethiopia and the Philippines, after changing his name from Tawil to the more Hebrew Tuval. I had first come across Tuval when he was still Tawil, deputy commander of the Jewish Quarter who negotiated the surrender with Major Abdullah Tel.

I was curious to hear what had happened to Major Tel from one who had had direct dealings with him. "Major Tel wasn't a fanatic back in 1948," Tuval said. "He may well have been influenced by Mousa el Husseini. Who knows? He was supposed to have been involved in the murder of King Abdullah and sought political asylum in Egypt, where he became an out-spoken Nasser supporter and bitterly denounced Jordan's policies. Years later he was pardoned by King Hussein and allowed to return to Jordan. There he died."

"Of natural causes?" I asked.

"Yes, but . . . There is a 'but,'" Tuval explained. "Everything that had happened to him in all those years affected his heart. He died of a heart attack. If you want to say 'of natural causes,' you are right."

After coffee was served, the conversation turned to the Jewish Quarter in 1948. Here are Shaul Tuval's recollections of the events leading up to the capitulation:

"I had been a teacher in the Jewish Quarter since 1945, and was allowed to travel freely from the New City to the Old City till the United Nations decision to partition Palestine in November 1947. For three days the Arabs stoned the Jews and burned their cars. That was the beginning of the siege and it led the Department of Education of the Jewish Agency to organize a staff of twenty teachers who would stay in the Old City to educate the children there. I took over this group after the man in charge was wounded.

"The Old City had become a very dangerous place. We conducted classes in two shifts—girls in the morning and boys in the afternoon. The aristocratic families, with the exception of the Weingartens, had left the Old City. One third of the population had moved out. We were down to about fourteen hundred people. The poor remained because they had nowhere else to go. I taught their children.

"Being a schoolteacher was only part of my work. I was also in charge of Gadna—a paramilitary youth brigade. We trained young people who then went into the Haganah at seventeen. I managed to raise a company of about a hundred boys and girls because, as a schoolteacher, both the parents and the pupils knew and trusted me. Of that company, about fifty were between the ages of fourteen and fifteen. They did marvelous things during the siege. About twenty-five were taken to POW camp in Jordan, so we opened a school for them there. But I'm getting ahead of

myself . . .

"On that fateful morning of May 28 I was at my headquarters at Sha'ar Hashamyin when Moshe Rusnak (page 116), in command of the Jewish Quarter, asked to see me at Batei Mahse. There I learned that Rabbi Hazan and Rabbi Mintzberg had gone to see Major Tel, who had told them, 'I'm not prepared to talk to you because you're civilians. You have nothing to do with this. Go back to your headquarters and report that I want to see a representative of the Haganah.' Then he sent Rabbi Hazan with the message, but kept Rabbi Mintzberg as a hostage.

"Rusnak said to me, 'We've decided to send you as the Haganah representative.' My instructions were to play for time, to hold out till nightfall in the hope that help was on the way. Rabbi Mordechai Weingarten, president of the Jewish community, was to come with me.

"We went straight from Rusnak's headquarters in Batei Mahse to Sha'ar Hashamyin, through Beit El to Rehov Ha Yehudim, and across no-man's-land to the Armenian Quarter. There Major Tel was waiting for us at Zion Gate, near the old Turkish wall.

"'Are you here to surrender?' he asked.

"As my instructions were to play for time by offering to negotiate a cease fire, I said to him, 'You have wounded. We have wounded. So I suggest a cease fire for half an hour or an hour . . .'

"Major Tel smiled. 'We don't need a cease fire,' he said. 'If you want to surrender, that's a different matter.'

"I told him that I didn't have any instructions to surrender, but if he wanted to give me his terms I'd transmit them to my headquarters, adding, 'If you want to talk about surrendering, Major Tel, we have to sit down and discuss the matter. We can't talk about it in the street.'

"Major Tel thought it over and said, 'Good.' We went to his advance headquarters in the Armenian monastery. According to King Abdullah's terms, we were to surrender and turn over our weapons. Those physically fit and of military age were to be taken prisoner. Three representatives—Major Tel, Rabbi Weingarten and myself—would decide who was a fighter, who would go to POW camp and who would be set free. Women, children and the aged would be allowed to cross over to the Israeli side in the New City. Anyone who wanted to stay in the Old City under the sovereignty of Abdullah was free to do so.

"He then gave me half an hour to get an answer. 'In half an hour I can't do anything,' I told him. 'We have to assemble the commanders. It takes time to negotiate a surrender.'

"By now it was around ten o'clock. Major Tel gave me till one. If we hadn't met his terms by then fighting would resume.

"On our way back, Weingarten and I crossed no-man's-land and were in the Street of the Jews when Arab soldiers started shooting. I ducked into a store and got separated from Weingarten. The soldiers ordered me to come out with my hands up and my back to them. Two legionnaires jumped me and took me prisoner. I was the first prisoner of war in all of Jerusalem. The two legionnaires felt they'd achieved something magnificent as they marched me along the Via Dolorosa to Major Tel's headquarters at the *rauda*, unaware he was in the Armenian Quarter at the time.

"Those two kilometers were my own Via Dolorosa. Threatening Arab crowds filled the streets. As it was close to prayer time, there were thousands of worshippers on their way to the mosque chanting 'The first prisoner! The first prisoner!' It was a very tense situation. Since the crowd looked as if it might get out of hand, the two legionnaires kept shouting, 'Anyone who touches him will get killed.'

"This was a very dangerous moment for me, and I'll tell you why. Before the war started I was the Haganah intelligence officer in the Old City. There were a number of people—Arabs and Armenians—I had made contact with and bought Sten guns from. As they had worked for me, they knew me well. Any one of them might have been in that crowd and killed me to protect himself.

"I had been in Major Tel's headquarters at the *rauda* for about fifteen minutes when Rabbi Weingarten arrived. He too had been captured by legion soldiers and brought there. Rabbi Weingarten was very agitated 'You see what's going on?' he shouted. 'We have to surrender!'

"'Please, Mr. Weingarten,' I said to him, 'a little calm, please. Neither you nor I will decide whether we surrender. That will be decided after we return—*if* we return. So, please, Mr. Weingarten, remain calm.'

"Soon after, Ahmed Hilmi Pasha, prime minister of the short-lived Palestine government, came in and said to me, 'What are *you* doing here?'

"I explained what had happened, adding, 'One of your soldiers took my watch. If the Arab Legion is a disciplined army, I want it back.' I think this impressed him—a POW talking about his watch. I may have looked calm, but actually I was nervous. I got my watch back on the spot. Then Ahmed Hilmi Pasha phoned Abdullah Tel at the Armenian Quarter. Tel said, 'Send him back.'

"I was driven to where the major was waiting for me. He was very angry. 'I know you're a spy,' he said. 'You wanted to spy on our headquarters. Go back to your people and tell them my terms. You have one hour.'

"I had managed to gain two hours through all of this business. Now I pressed for more time. 'Major Tel,' I said, 'you know how armies operate. I must have time to explain all the details you've given me.'

"Tel thought it over and said, 'I give you till four o'clock.'

"By 1:00 P.M. I was back at my headquarters and all the commanders were reassembled. Not all of them agreed to surrender, although most did. 'We have no option,' was the consensus. The Arab Legion had been moving closer to our positions during this lull. They were now meters away from our refugee center in the synagogue, where there were about a thousand civilians. When the Arabs started shooting, Rusnak asked me to go and tell the major we would not negotiate till his soldiers fell back to their original positions.

"I left the meeting and went back to the Arab lines for the second time that day, not knowing what the outcome would be. It was almost four o'clock when Weingarten joined me and said the headquarters staff had now decided to surrender. Together we went toward Zion Gate, where the surrender terms were signed by Rusnak and Major Tel. Also present were Mousa el Husseini, a nephew of the Grand Mufti, and the United Nations representative, Dr. Pablo de Azcarate.

"When we went into Batei Mahse to implement the surrender terms, Major Tel said to me, 'Where are the weapons you have to turn over?' After he saw that we had so few of them—some Sten guns, automatic weapons, rifles, revolvers and a two-inch mortar—he got very angry. 'If I'd known this was your situation, I swear I would have conquered you with sticks,' he said. Then, when he saw we had only thirty-five soldiers, he got even angrier. 'Sixteen days of fighting for thirty-five POWs! That's impossible!' he shouted. This is the reason he took away about four hundred prisoners.

"Some tried to escape. One of my platoon commanders, a fellow named Abraham Yefit, went to the hospital, took bandages, and wrapped them around his hands and neck. When Major Tel and I were checking over the prisoners, Yefit stood there sighing and crying. 'What have we here?' Tel asked as he took the bandages off Yefit, who was playing the part of a seriously wounded man. When Tel saw he was not wounded at all, he kicked him. This incident gave Tel the impression there were other such actors among us. As a result he took away many who were really wounded.

"After Tel left, an Iraqi officer led me to the Armenian Quarter to question me about the Old City, the people, the weapons. He interrogated me till midnight, then took me to the *kishleh* to join the other prisoners. According to international law, those who negotiate a surrender are not made prisoner. But somebody else took advantage of this privilege while I was being questioned and went free instead."

"My father was what you'd call today a Zionist," said Moshe Rusnak, administrator at Hadassah hospital. "I am not a Zionist. Zionism was born only fifty years ago. I am a Jew. And if I'm a Jew I cannot be a Zionist. Jews were coming to Israel long before Zionism. Even if Hertzl had never been born, I would have come. What does Zionism mean anyway? Every Jew who prays, prays every day. He wants to come and see Zion. Zion means Jerusalem . . . Mount Zion." Rusnak and I were seated on the steps of Rothschild House, in what had been called Ashkenazi Square at the time of the siege. As we talked, a group of tourists entered the square. Their guide told them about the historic siege of the Jewish Quarter. The tourists didn't notice the slim man in the straw hat seated on the steps. Even if they had, they would never have known he was Moshe Rusnak, the Haganah officer in command of the Jewish Quarter during the days of the battle.

"I was listed as a doctor and sent into the Old City in December 1947," Rusnak continued after the tourists had left. "The British police were told that a doctor must be sent to the Old City. They gave me an ambulance and an escort of two armed vehicles. I drove the ambulance. Going into the Old City officially as a doctor made me nervous, as I didn't even know basic first aid. Fortunately, nobody asked me to take care of them.

"The minute I got into the Old City I went underground. We had about one hundred people, thirteen rifles, about fifteen or twenty submachine guns and thirty revolvers. The breakthrough brought us about sixty more men, but they were not fighters. They were supposed to bring supplies into the Old City and take the wounded out. But they stayed on. All told we had one hundred fairly well-trained people with very little equipment. During the last days of the battle we buried forty-eight and left behind two . . . five . . . eight more bodies. We had about two hundred wounded.

"In the end there were about thirty lightly wounded fighters standing on their feet.

"Major Tel told me to reassemble everyone so he could separate them into combatant and noncombatant groups. He took some old people who were seventy, and I can assure you he took boys of twelve and thirteen. Altogether he took about three hundred, including some wounded. It so happened that some seriously wounded people went to prison while some lightly wounded were sent out to the New City. There was even an old beggar who was taken to prison camp.

"I was in the Old City from December 1947 until the end of May 1948. I will never forget those six months as long as I live. After all these years I can't forget. It's not easy to explain. Maybe a writer could express those emotions. Not me. I am not a poet or an author. Dostoevsky could take one hundred pages to express a feeling that actually lasted only one or two minutes. I can't do it."

Yaacov Kastel works for Jerusalem's electric company. He is in charge of pruning trees that encroach on the electric lines along the streets.

Kastel was born in Hebron, but his family moved to Jerusalem after the 1929 pogrom. Kastel's father, a deeply religious man, dreamed of his son becoming a rabbi or cantor. "I was headed in that direction," Kastel told me, "but at the age of sixteen I was drafted by the Gadna, the paramilitary youth organization under the Haganah, and somehow I got away from religion."

Yaacov Kastel was a member of the Jewish Quarter's original garrison. The first time he held a rifle was during the siege. The first time he fired it was at an onrushing Arab.

Yitzhak Ishai, the dark-haired youth I photographed in a hospital ward twenty-seven years ago, had become a balding middle-aged customs officer. A gregarious person, Yitzhak gossiped cheerily about the survivors of the siege and told me how successful they had become. He recognized most of them in my pictures. All were married and had children, with the exception of Meir Alcotzer (page 74), a confirmed bachelor.

To Ishai's knowledge, there was only one tragic story—that of Shlomo Zadok. Shlomo had been a friend of his. They had grown up together in the Jewish Quarter. "Shlomo was very gentle," Yitzhak sighed. "I'll never understand why an Arab soldier hit him on the back of his head with a rifle butt as we were being led off to prison. Shlomo never recovered from that blow. He suffered from nerves and severe depressions.

"After we got back from prison camp he went to work, but was soon sent to a mental hospital. In time they released him, but after that it was in and out, in and out. His mother was a family friend. She frequently visited my mother. One day she brought Shlomo along. He was very quiet. Soon after they left, Shlomo came back alone. He asked my mother for a glass of water. As she was returning from the kitchen, Shlomo threw himself off the fifth-floor balcony."

120

Yehoshua Levy, press director of the *Jerusalem Post*, stopped to speak with one of his typesetters. Levy has worked on this English-language daily since the time it was called the *Palestine Post*.

When the fighting broke out he was assistant manager and, as a key executive, had been deferred from military duty. However, Yehoshua wanted to be assigned to a combat unit because he reasoned that, if the situation in Jerusalem became really critical, the paper would not come out anyway and he would not be needed in his civilian role.

"One night the electric power failed," he told me. "It was two in the morning before we cut a stencil edition. 'Got to go and do something,' I said to myself after the paper was put to bed. I went to a post where I found Benshemesh (page 128) and two others. At about nine in the morning we got a phone call. Volunteers were needed for a job in the Old City of Jerusalem for about twenty-four hours. Since the newspaper office would probably be without electricity for at least a day or two, I felt free to go. Benshemesh and I volunteered.

"Since my father didn't have a telephone, I was unable to notify him that I was going into the Old City and, as nobody at the post bothered to make a list of our names, there was no record of who had volunteered. The only official information was that a group had gone into the Old City to fight. As far as my family was concerned, I had disappeared. They thought I had been killed.

"I did almost die. After the surrender an Arab irregular grabbed me as we were being marched off to prison camp. He was dragging me into a narrow alley to kill me, when a legionnaire saved my life. He shot him down. Just like that!"

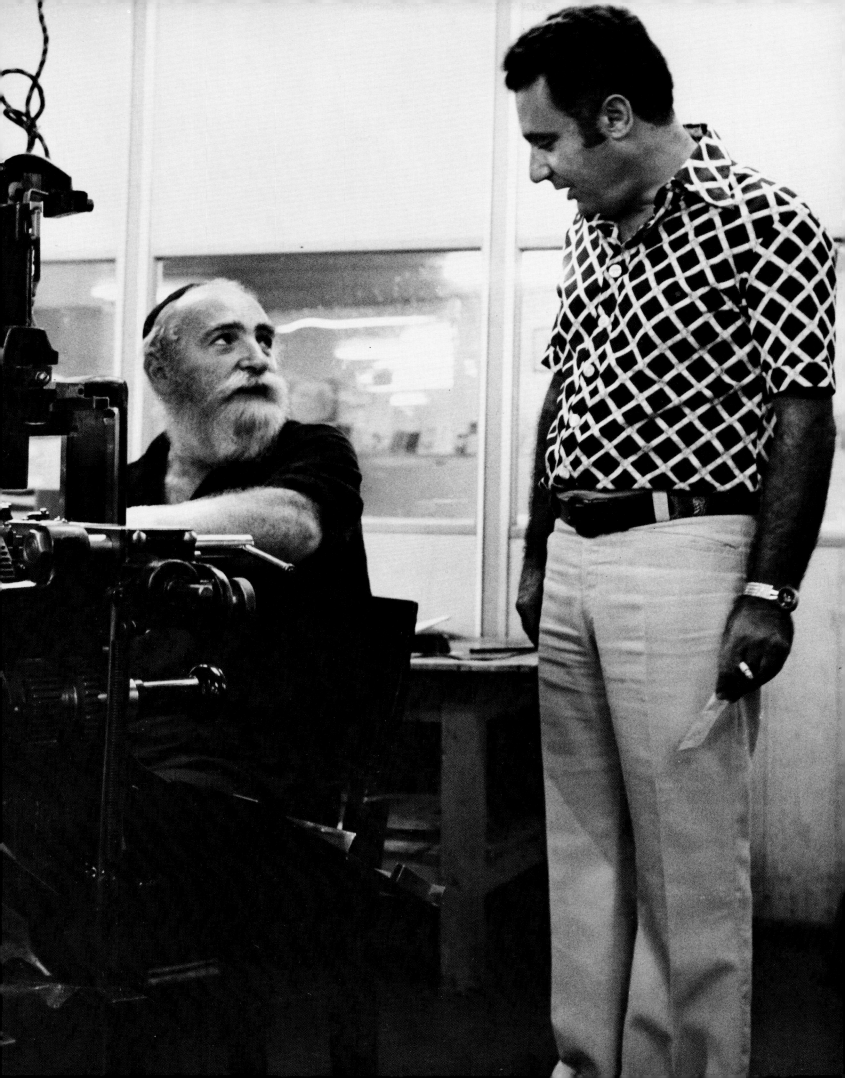

Mordechai Yona was born in Jerusalem. Like most young Palestinians of his generation, he has had his share of excitement.

In 1947 Yona joined the Haganah, while one of his brothers became a member of the Stern Gang. On a February afternoon in 1948, Yona strolled down Ben Yehuda Street minutes before a pro-Arab British deserter killed more than fifty people by setting off three truckloads of explosives. This terrorist scheme to break Jewish morale had been conceived by Abdel Kader el Husseini, on orders of the Mufti. Six weeks later Yona took part in a battle at Castel, an old Roman fort controlling the road to Jerusalem, where Abdel Kader led the charge. Yona fought alongside Sergeant Major Meir Karmion, who killed Abdel Kader during the assault.

Yona was later sent into the Jewish Quarter. A bomb exploded, killing several fighters near him, but he only got nicked by a ricochet. Then the building in which he was posted received a direct hit. Yona suffered a concussion from falling debris. Taken prisoner, he was among those who spent the night at the old Turkish prison near Jaffa Gate. Brandishing swords, Arab civilians threatened to murder them. In Jordan, Yona faced jeers and more threats as he and other prisoners were placed on exhibit in front of the local population before being shipped on to POW camp.

Today Yona, fifteen pounds heavier, is administrative assistant in the Department of Foreign Relations of the Jewish Agency in Jerusalem. He is a television devotee. His favorite program is "Kojak."
"What appeals to you about that show?" I asked him.
"The excitement," Yona said.

Shlomo Kubi, the relief stationmaster on the Palestinian Railways, boarded the 5:30 out of Jerusalem on the morning of Saturday, November 29, 1947. A native of the Golan Heights, near the Syrian border, Kubi had joined the Palestinian civil service in 1920. According to his schedule that morning, Kubi was to relieve the Arab stationmaster at the village of Batir, then proceed to Deir Elsheikh on Sunday, Wadi Sarrar on Monday, Hartuv on Tuesday and Ramla on Wednesday. Little did Kubi suspect when he boarded the 5:30 that his twenty-eight years of active duty in the civil service under the British mandate of Palestine would end that same day.

By the time the 5:30 pulled into Batir, news of the impending UN vote on the partition of Palestine had reached that Arab village. Rioting had broken out. A prudent man, Kubi remained aboard the train until it reached Deir Elsheikh. He expected to be put up there by a friendly Arab family with whom he always stayed. The extent of the family's hospitality on that particular day was to recommend a room with a strong lock someplace where Kubi would probably be safe in the event the populace burned the station. Kubi pushed on. Finding the situation equally explosive in Wadi Sarrar, he decided to go on to Hartuv, a Jewish settlement. From there he made his way back to Jerusalem and reached his home in the Old City, thanks to a lift in a British police car.

Once inside the Jewish Quarter, Kubi remained there until the surrender. He acted as sanitary inspector for the duration. When the fighters and civilians were lined up in Rothschild Square and divided into two groups—prisoners of war or evacuees—Kubi instinctively fell in with the civilians until he saw Major Tel direct his fifteen-year-old son Rami to the POW line-up. "They're taking my son!" Kubi thought. "I must go with him."

As he and Rami stood among the prisoners, Kubi caught sight of his wife Judith and their daughter Shoshana standing with the refugees across the square.

"I felt in my heart," Kubi recalled, "that I had to take care of them as well. So I looked around. As I didn't see Major Tel, and no one else was watching us, Rami and I left the prisoners and joined the group of evacuees who were to be sent out of the Old City."

After the war the Jerusalem–Tel Aviv line was temporarily out of service, because the bridges were down. Kubi, now a civil servant in the Israeli government, was transferred to Haifa and became its stationmaster in 1949.

Shimon Benshemesh, a Sabra born in Haifa, is today the director general and chief executive of the Jewish National Fund. This organization was founded in 1901 at the Fifth Zionist Congress, held in Basel. Its purpose was to purchase land in Palestine. Next to the government, the Jewish National Fund owns most of the public land in Israel today, and is responsible for its development. Land reclamation, road building and forestation are among Benshemesh's responsibilities. Since 1948, for instance, the Jewish National Fund has planted 130,000,000 pines and cypresses. These trees, however, do not prevent Mr. Benshemesh from seeing the forest. As we sat in his Jerusalem office he gave me a clear picture of the siege, the surrender, and what occurred thereafter.

"On May 17 we were gathered together on short notice from various parts of Jerusalem as auxiliaries. We didn't know each other, or why we were being assembled. In the evening we were brought to Yemin Moshe, from where you can see the old walled city across the wadi and, to the right, the Church of the Dormition on Mount Zion. During the night we crossed the wadi and went up the hill to Mount Zion until we came to Zion Gate, which leads into the Old City.

"The Palmach led the operation. They blasted through Zion Gate and we entered the Jewish Quarter carrying ammunition and medical supplies. Then they left and, in my humble opinion—I'm not an army general—that was a bitter mistake. They should have stayed, at least for a few days. We were not well prepared, from the military point of view, and we were left alone with the remnants of the Jewish Quarter's population. Our own families had not been notified. For days they looked for us before discovering we were in the Old City.

"By morning we found ourselves in the ruins of the Jewish Quarter, face to face with the Syrian irregulars and the Arab Legion. We fought from door to door. Never in my life will I forget the spirit of the civilians, especially the younger generation. They took tin cans, filled them with nails and a bit of gunpowder, and gave them to us to use as grenades against the Arabs.

"As the Arabs didn't fight at night, we could relax in the evening. But during the day we were attacked without interruption. They shelled us from the Mount of Olives. There was no way to escape. Day after day we had more casualties. The underground hospital was filled with more and more wounded. Medical supplies dropped lower and lower. We asked for help from the outside. We knew the Palmach had tried once or twice to break through again. The Arab Legion was closing in on us until we were really within their grasp. They were so close we could actually see that every legionnaire was fully equipped and loaded down with ammunition.

"Here I want to mention the spirit of the Jewish population and give you an example of how united

they were. Four or five days after we came into the Old City we celebrated a small religious festival. I don't remember now in which synagogue it was held, but I'll never forget the lights of the candles or the devotion of the elderly as they sat together, danced together, and prayed together. We all behaved as though everything were normal, you see. The people didn't touch anything that wasn't 100 percent kosher, even though the enemy was only yards away.

"It was decided to surrender after we stopped getting any affirmative answers to our calls for help. We surrendered because the Arab Legion, under the command of King Abdullah, stood on the other side of the Old City wall. Knowing his character and his way of dealing with such matters in the past, it was our hope that we would not be slaughtered on surrendering.

"After the Arab Legion received our signals they came down and discovered the small group of defenders left. A legion officer said, 'If we'd known this we'd have come after you with our spiked hats'—you know, those Arab Legion helmets which look a bit like the German *Pickelhaube*," Benshemesh smiled. "We were then taken to the *kishleh*, the old Turkish prison near Jaffa Gate, and held there until dark. The idea was to get us through the Arab Quarter and on our way to Jordan while everyone was asleep because, if we'd been taken through during the day, even the legion couldn't have prevented the mobs from massacring us.

"We left as dawn broke over the Old City. The Jewish Quarter was in flames. I prayed to God my family didn't know I had been there, because they would have thought I was dead. By some miracle it took days before my family found out I had been in the Old City. A good friend of mine in the Foreign Office who knew that I had been in the Old City went immediately to take my wife and little daughter to his home in Rehavia, a residential district of Jerusalem. He didn't tell my wife I'd been in the Jewish Quarter until he received news from me. Meanwhile, he made arrangements to have my wife and daughter sent out of Jerusalem. The authorities were evacuating everyone who wasn't essential, because the population was almost at the point of starvation.

"My wife was in Haifa with her family when she got the news that I was a prisoner. Before I was taken to the *kishleh* I had scribbled a message on the back of one of my law certificates, which I stuffed into an empty pack of cigarettes. Then I asked a school-teacher who was being evacuated to the New City to deliver the message to my wife. That's how she found out I was alive.

"We were taken to a POW camp in Mafraq, twenty-five miles northeast of Amman. Of course, the Arab soldiers who escorted us took everything they could. They took our watches . . . they took our eyeglasses . . . but they didn't take our lives.

"The Arab camp commander was good to us. He would turn up the radio in his tent on the other side of the fence so that we could listen in. Shaul Tuval, who was fluent in Arabic, used to sit near the fence and pick up the messages. Tuval also listened to the hidden radio we had bought from the Arabs, and would give us his interpretation of the news. This was most important to us.

"By order of King Abdullah the women and the aged were sent back to Israel after two or three days. Even though we received information on the first day of arrival at camp that we should be prepared to return home, we divided ourselves into five groups and established priorities as to the order in which each group would leave.

"We established an absolutely independent society with a general council and . . . I would say . . . our own prime minister. Everything possible in the life of the community was dealt with, from sharing our Red Cross supplies to deciding whether we would allow anyone to escape from the camp. There was even a court of appeals.

"During the first days at camp our military continued in command, but within a fortnight or so the leadership came out of the tents. It happened that during a discussion I objected to a certain point as a citizen of the camp. I objected to a resolution given by the commander, and they accepted my opinion. A day or so later I was asked to participate as a member of the council. It may sound like a joke, but, after the civil leadership had been established, the military commanders started a revolt. They couldn't stand it. It was all settled in twelve hours. We ceased being a military group. They had to step aside. It's remarkable how a new leadership emerged, even during such distressing times.

"The council was made up of representatives from the tents. Each member of the council represented about a dozen or so men. Ours was an ad hoc council, really democratic. Everybody understood it was the best way. We had different forms of behavior because we came from different parts of the country and different ways of life: the elderly people from the Old City—the Sephardim, the Ashkenazi—and the younger people who came from the *kibbutzim*. It was amazing how we managed to live together in a closed society in those unhappy days. We knew that the older people needed more cigarettes because they were accustomed to them, so we persuaded the young people to allot extra money for this purpose. In this way the older people could pass the dark and sad days more easily.

"I would say—and I'm glad to say it—that the Arab Legion was honest. They behaved correctly. It's normal in prisoner-of-war camps, especially in the East, that every parcel is stolen by the guards. I don't think we had many cases of this. It's usual, of course. But I don't think that this even occurred.

"Now, with the help of God really, and the dry weather of Mafraq—it's a desert, you see—almost every wound healed very quickly. It was really a blessing from God.

"Pessimists said that we would never go back home, that they would finish us off slowly, group by group, as they wished. I was very optimistic and, politically, I was right. I knew there was a big difference between King Abdullah and the Syrians. The Syrians were very cruel. Now, if I'm not mistaken, we were imprisoned for nine months, a relatively short period of time. It would have been very easy for them to say, 'Excuse us, but you'll work here till the end of your days.' But we even had some good times. As I said, the aged, the women and children were sent home almost immediately, so we already had an indication that they were not going to be bestial. By means of the radio we knew there were negotiations going on between Major Abdullah Tel and Moshe Dayan.

"I got back home with the fourth group and went straight to my office at the Jewish National Fund. The situation was not so simple with respect to my daughter, who was only nine months old when I left home and wouldn't recognize me. I said to myself, 'Don't take your daughter in your arms and display too much emotion. She won't understand. She can't remember you. You're a stranger to her.' So I bought some candy and behaved as if I were some relative who'd come to see her. But she's a clever girl. Later my wife came to me and told me that when she was putting her to bed she said, 'You know, this uncle is a very nice uncle.'

"You want to know my feelings about the Old City?" Benshemesh asked. "Coming back to the Old City was something I can't explain. It was tremendously emotional. All the warriors of the Jewish Quarter met there. I went from one ruin to another. I remembered the places where my friends fell near me . . . and the place where the prayerful were gathered . . . I remembered where the bullets came at me . . . I remembered everything. You touch the wings of history at such a time. But now it's gone. It's not the same any more. I don't feel like going back there." Benshemesh paused before going on. "From time to time I wonder . . . Is it better, in a historical sense, to be killed defending your interests, or to surrender and return to start again? Now, it's fruitless to be killed just for the demonstration of it. Humbly speaking, since the surrender I have raised my family—a boy and a girl who have served honorably in our army. I can talk to you about the beauty of Jerusalem, about what we've accomplished at the Jewish National Fund, this public institute which is dedicated to forestation, land policies, and fighting hunger. I think all this is better than being a corpse."

At Sheik Bader, on the outskirts of Jerusalem, there is an abandoned cemetery only accessible by foot. It became a cemetery in 1948 after the Mount of Olives, and its Jewish cemetery, was taken over by Jordan. Sheik Bader was only used until late in 1951. By then many graves had been removed to new and more conveniently located cemeteries.

There were still 3,400 people buried at Sheik Bader when I got there in search of the graves of Rabbi Israel Zelig Kaniel and his wife Eidel. They were the old couple I'd photographed climbing slowly up a hill to Batei Mahse on their way to Ashkenazi Square to be evacuated to an old people's home in the New City. There they would die before the Mount of Olives became Israeli territory and consequently would not be buried in the Jewish cemetery, as they had always expected.

I had no idea where the graves were located when I started my search. There was no caretaker to guide me. Since I cannot read Hebrew, I enlisted the help of a young Israeli. We went methodically from one grave to another, from one row of graves to another, from one end of the cemetery to the other. I do not know how many gravestones we peered at on that hot and dusty August afternoon before we found the grave of Mrs. Eidel Kaniel, who died in the Hebrew year 5710. Several hundred graves later we came upon her husband's last resting place. Rabbi Kaniel had died in the year 5711.

Mordechai Gazit, soldier and diplomat, is a soft-spoken, imperturbable man. Whenever he says "Sorry . . ." it is the closest he comes to losing his temper. Gazit can be so punctilious that, during the Sinai negotiations, in which he participated as political advisor to the Israeli prime minister, he is said to have driven Joseph Sisco, the U.S. assistant secretary of state, up the wall. Henry Kissinger nicknamed him Mr. Dot the I's and Cross the T's. Now a retired general, Gazit was equally unflappable in combat. During the 1948 War of Independence Gazit, then a company commander, was ordered to relieve the Palmach—the elite force—which was about to break through Zion Gate to reinforce the Jewish Quarter and bring in supplies on the night of May 18. He was given ninety-seven untrained men who had been picked at random an hour earlier. Mordechai Gazit recalled these events as he sat in a reception room of the Israeli Foreign Office in Jerusalem beneath the portraits of past secretaries of state Abba Eban, Golda Meir and Moshe Sharett.

"What happened is a rather strange and interesting story," he said. "The first thing we had to do was get my ninety-seven men more or less organized as a company and take their names. This we did before we went to Yemin Moshe, a suburb of Jerusalem from where we were to set off. While my men were assembling, I attended a commanders' conference. The senior officer there made two points. First, his men would break through Zion Gate into the Armenian Quarter. They would then mop up whatever there was to mop up, thereby—and I'm quoting him now—'solving the problem of the whole city once and for all.' In other words, he would link the Old City and the New, reuniting Jerusalem. He made it all sound very easy. I was impressed, even though I felt that he came from another planet and that, frankly, he didn't know what he was talking about. My assessment of the situation was quite different from his with respect to what could and could not be accomplished in Jerusalem, since I had seen the fighting there for several months. I said to myself, 'If he has the necessary forces, the necessary confidence, the necessary equipment and the necessary morale, then by all means . . .' But I had my doubts about that.

"Then he made his second point: 'You will enter the Old City with your people and stay in the Jewish Quarter.'

"'Sorry . . .' I said, 'my instructions are to relieve your people on Mount Zion. I'm not supposed to go into the Jewish Quarter, especially as my men haven't got the proper training or the right weapons. They aren't equipped for fighting in urban areas.'

"'You will do as I say,' he told me.

"'I'm not taking orders from you,' I said. 'I have my own chain of command.'

"'Phone your people,' he told me, 'and you'll see there's been a reversal of orders.'

"I did, and was told: 'You will enter the Old City and stay there.'

134

"'My people are a voluntary army and they may refuse to do it,' I said. 'They may even mutiny. They are married men, only sons, orphans, and I don't know what all.'

"'Well, try and talk to them. Give them a pep talk,' I was told.

"'I'll do that!' I said. Then I asked, 'What am I supposed to do once I enter the Old City?'

"I was a fighting officer, having graduated from officers' training school four years earlier. Once I entered the old quarter I would be the ranking officer. I took that for granted, not because I was terribly ambitious, but because this had happened to me once before when I'd been sent to the Jewish Quarter without clear instructions, in December 1947. And I don't like to be in ill-defined situations. I hate that sort of thing. I don't mind not doing anything, but if I'm sent somewhere I want to know precisely what I'm expected to do. After my previous experience, I didn't want the same thing to happen again.

"'You'll be the special representative of the Jerusalem area commander,' I was told.

"'What do you mean by that?' I asked.

"'There is a civilian population there. You will lift their morale,' I was told.

"'I'm not a morale lifter!' I said. 'I am a fighting officer.' But, as I knew the situation was critical, I said to myself, 'Okay, I'll go and make speeches.' I didn't relish what I had to do.

"At around eleven that night we started moving up from Yemin Moshe to Mount Zion. There was no road, so it was a steep climb. My ninety-seven men carried about thirty kilos of plasma and ammunition apiece on their backs. The moon was shining and, in my opinion, it was a perfect case of mismanagement. Fortunately, the Arabs were somewhat confused after the battle of the night before and we reached the top of Mount Zion without mishap.

"There I was confronted by a relaxed young officer. 'You're to relieve my men on the mount,' he told me.

"'Sorry . . .' I said, 'I am supposed to enter the Old City.'

"'No, you will relieve my men on the mount,' he repeated.

"'Okay, I'll relieve your men,' I said. 'Now we're back where we started.'

"I decided to put eighty men in position and keep seventeen with me as runners, so that if I needed the eighty in a hurry I could round them up. Nothing happened for hours. Midnight . . . one . . . two . . . three. No one said a word. The men we had relieved were sleeping on the ground, exhausted.

"Someone woke them up, reassembled them, and said, 'Fellows, I know you are dead tired. We shall not expect anything from you beyond what you can do. You still have to break through Zion Gate and get into the Old City. That's all.'

"'What about breaking through into the Armenian Quarter and the mopping up operation, which was supposed to be the solution to the problem of linking the New and the Old City?' I asked myself.

"I walked up to the chief of operations and said, 'I want to know what is happening. I have ninety-seven men here.'

"He took me to the command post as the attack started. After the breakthrough he said to me, 'Now quick, take your men into the Jewish Quarter.'

"'My dear fellow,' I explained, 'my men are scattered all over Mount Zion.'

"'Yes, yes,' he said, 'but get them into the Old City quick.'

"There was no point in arguing, because I had debated this in my own mind for the last four hours. I knew this was going to be a nice kettle of fish. So I sent twelve of my seventeen runners to round up my men but didn't wait for them all to regroup. I went back and forth from Zion Gate to the Jewish Quarter five or six times. On the last trip the chief of operations, who had asked me to move into the Jewish Quarter, walked up to me and said, 'You will now occupy Zion Gate.'

"'What do you mean, occupy Zion Gate?' I said. 'I only have four men left here with me. All the others are in the Jewish Quarter.'

"'Okay, I'll do it,' he said.

"It was natural to me that they would do it. They were in position and holding Zion Gate. I went outside, found my four men and some more ammunition, walked back inside, and that was it.

"Now, as I entered the Old City, there was excitement and a feeling of relief among the populace. An officer came up to me, someone I didn't know. 'Where do you come from?' he demanded. 'Why did you come? Who needs you?'

"'Do you think I'm here for my pleasure?' I asked him.

"'Go and occupy the Armenian Quarter,' he said.

"The Armenian Quarter, which dominated the Jewish Quarter, was a serious military headache. So I said, 'You know something? I'll occupy the Armenian Quarter! Just show me the way and I'm with you.'

"That settled it, because he didn't have the men to do it.

"By then my ninety-seven men had been sent to reinforce the different positions and give the men there a chance to get some sleep. From that point of view, at least, they were being useful. But they certainly no longer existed as a unit. It might have proved interesting to get my ninety-seven men together again, but it would not have served any purpose. They were in the Jewish Quarter to be useful. I looked around the command post and found that there was a reserve unit which could be activated whenever there was an attack. This was good to know.

"At about ten o'clock in the morning I was told that a youngster who had entered through Zion Gate with us, bringing some chickens to relatives in the Jewish Quarter, had tried to go back to the New City but was unable to, because the Arab Legion had taken over the gate. It had not been held as the chief of operations had led me to believe it would. It had been abandoned so that, when Glubb Pasha's company arrived, they just took it over without our being aware of it until the boy tried to leave. This meant that, instead of twelve hundred potential victims of a massacre in the Jewish Quarter, there would now be thirteen hundred.

"In Glubb Pasha's book, *A Soldier with the Arabs*, there's a description of how he sent a company into the Old City, because he thought we would take it over. At one o'clock they launched their attack. And they came at us, a perfectly well-trained regular army against men who hadn't slept and were not well-trained. I called out the reserve unit and, to make myself generally useful, headed the counterattack. We repulsed them. We even took a small machine gun.

"At the synagogue of Yochanan Ben Zakkai there were people praying feverishly. 'What are you so desperate about?' I asked them. 'We have just defeated the Arabs.' They were rather happy to hear that, but not all that happy. They remained skeptical about the situation.

"I went into a house, which had a tiled roof, to survey the situation and heard cries behind me: 'Don't do that! It's dangerous!' Obviously it was dangerous. There wasn't anything that wasn't! So that didn't impress me very much. As I reached the roof I saw a big hole in the tiles. I looked out towards the Cathedral of St. James in the Armenian Quarter and, before I could really enjoy the beautiful view, I received two or three bullets from a machine gun on the spire of that very church. A woman soldier shouted, 'The commander is wounded!' as I lost consciousness . . ."

Israel Hashmonai was born in the Old City. On the day it fell, the world he knew lay in shambles. Hashmonai and his father were prisoners of war. His mother and two sisters, evicted from their homes, were refugees. No wonder Hashmonai paid little attention to Allenby Bridge the first time he crossed it on his way to prison camp in Jordan. But "it was a misty morning, at 6:30 A.M., on May 29, 1948," Hashmonai remembers with the total recall of a customs inspector.

With equal accuracy Hashmonai remembers when he re-crossed Allenby Bridge on his return from prison camp. "It was a very dark morning, at 4:30 A.M., on March 31, 1949," he told me. One hour and thirty minutes later Hashmonai reached Mandelbaum Gate in Jerusalem, then the border point between Jordan and Israel.

Two years, eight months and sixteen days later, on December 16, 1951, to be exact, Israel Hashmonai was assigned to Mandelbaum Gate as a sergeant in the customs police. For the next sixteen years he was in charge of the Israeli side. For the last seven of these sixteen he held a daily conference with his Jordanian vis-a-vis, Sergeant Fatim Abu Ahmed. Each morning at 8:00 A.M. they would discuss the number of visitors who would cross the border that day. The pair also pampered such dignitaries as Mrs. Eleanor Roosevelt and Pope Paul VI.

After the Six Day War in 1967, Mandelbaum Gate was no longer Jerusalem's border point between Israel and Jordan. Hashmonai was assigned to Allenby Bridge—now the key crossing on the West Bank—with the rank of deputy inspector. (Sergeant Fatim Abu Ahmed of Jordanian Customs, having opted to remain in Jerusalem, became Lieutenant Fatim Abu Ahmed of Israeli Customs.)

Today Hashmonai spends six months a year at Allenby and six months at Adam Bridge (opposite page), twenty-five miles north of Jericho. Instead of the trickle of tourists that once drifted through Mandelbaum, the two bridges now handle a million visitors a year.

"Arabs residing abroad can visit Israel if they are Palestinians," Hashmonai explained as we sat in his office, while busloads of them cleared customs outside. "How do we know if a visitor is a Palestinian?" Hashmonai said, repeating my question. "He must have a member of his family living here to vouch for him. We then grant him a 30-day visitor's permit. If he wants to stay longer he can renew his permit. Moslems living here can travel abroad for as long as they like."

For the first time since 1948, Israeli goods are traveling to Arab countries. "Naturally, the Arabs still boycott Israeli merchandise," Hashmonai smiled, "but that doesn't prevent Arabs in Israel from shipping oranges out to Jordan, for example, from where they are then distributed to all the Moslem countries as Arab goods."

Benjamin Yanir was born in Cracow, Poland. He was eight years old when the family emigrated to Palestine.

In 1957, at the age of thirty, Yanir moved again. A promising young lawyer who earned his degree in Jerusalem, he decided to start his practice in Beersheba, a sleepy Biblical town that showed promise of growing rapidly into an industrial, educational and administrative center as Bedouins and camels gave way to modern concrete buildings. Yanir's law practice grew up with the new Beersheba as the population increased from 30,000 to 100,000 in less than twenty years. I visited him there, and he showed me the modern town hall and synagogue while he reminisced about the surrender of the Old City twenty-seven years before.

"Most of us didn't talk about whether we'd be killed or not. We were stunned. There were bitter discussions about whether we should surrender. Some said it was better not to. Everybody realized there were twelve hundred civilians in the Old City.

"My post was at a window three meters away from the gates of Yochanan Ben Zakkai synagogue, where the civilians were concentrated. It was the most secure place in the Jewish Quarter, just like an air-raid shelter. One thing was clear. There was not the slightest chance of our survival if the fighting went on that day.

"I was not so sure my life would be spared after we surrendered. I was not sure that the legion soldiers escorting us through the small streets could protect us from the howling civilian Arab mobs. The day after we surrendered, the Arab Legion took us in open buses from one Jordan village to another. At the center of these villages a legionnaire would shoot into the air to attract the population. They spat on us and threw stones. It was only after we got to prison camp and saw the Red Cross that I felt safe."

"I was made in Jerusalem," Pinchas Oestreicher explained as we sat in his workshop on Yad Charutzim. Pinchas has a flair for real estate. He bought property on Yad Charutzim at the time Jordan was just across the street. The neighborhood was under continual Arab fire, so the property went for nothing. After the Six Day War, the Jordanian border was moved back twenty miles to the West Bank, and Pinchas' property soared in value.

Oestreicher's father came from Hungary, and one can detect in Pinchas a jaunty panache generally associated with Budapest, when he recalls his career. "I was twenty-six when I joined the Haganah in 1948," he said. "At first, they put me in a squad that escorted truck convoys from Jerusalem to Tel Aviv. My father owned one of the largest mechanic shops in Jerusalem. I had made some Sten guns in my father's shop, so I was put to work on a mortar called the Davidka that we made out of pipes and other things.

"Some time after that, I was called up and issued a rifle. We were told we must reinforce the boys who were fighting in the Old City. I was with the group that broke through into the Jewish Quarter with medical supplies and ammunition. I was the first to go in and, as I was wearing an oversized U.S. Naval artillery helmet, the women started kissing me and jumping around. They thought I was the commanding officer.

"Actually, my commanding officer was Mordechai Gazit. He told me to come with him. He had a Mauser and a Molotov cocktail. We went to an alley near the Street of the Jews. There was an Arab Legion attack. Suddenly a legionnaire shot at us with a tommy gun. Gazit was hit by three bullets in the chest. I started shouting for a medic. Somebody came with a stretcher and we took him to the hospital. They had many wounded in a small room with an oil lamp. Dr. Riss was there, and Dr. Lauffer. Three or four doctors were there. I had sentiments towards this Gazit. He was a nice fellow. I thought he was kaput—finished. I went to one of the doctors and asked him to do something. He started shouting at me, 'There are many, many wounded, and this man is dead!'

"I said, 'He's not dead. His blood is still running.' I smeared some of the blood on the doctor's face and said, 'Look, there's his blood.'

They started working on Gazit. I am told I shouted. I don't remember what. And for a very long time I didn't know what became of him.

"Many years after the fall of the Old City and my return from POW camp, I had a workshop in town. A fellow wearing a dark grey suit came in to see me about a broken jack. He looked familiar to me. 'Don't I know you?' I asked him. It was ten years after the 1948 war, around 1958 or something like that. 'Tell me,' I said, 'where do I know you from? Your face is familiar.' I asked his name.

"'Mordechai Gazit,' he said.

"I said, 'Yes, Mordechai Weinstein!' In Yiddish *wein*

means 'wine' and *stein* is 'stone.' *Gazit* is a special kind of stone. He had changed his name to Hebrew. "He was our ambassador in Washington at the time. Then he came back and was the head of the Foreign Office here, under Abba Eban. Then Golda Meir took him as a secretary and advisor. He then became political advisor to Prime Minister Yitzhak Rabin and negotiated the Sinai Agreement with Kissinger. Now he's Israel's ambassador to France. And his life was in my hands when I took him to the hospital!

"After Gazit was hit, my CO was Nisan Zeldes, who is now a professor at the university. He was liked by everybody. Zeldes had three wounds in his legs, but that didn't stop him from getting around.

"We fought on for ten days. My stomach did the rhumba. I wasn't used to killing. I would speak to a fellow and the next thing I knew he would fall dead. At first I was afraid. Then I got used to it. I knew I had no alternative. I had to fight. Otherwise I would die for nothing. We were like rats running from hole to hole. The Arabs had a system. They blew up the houses around us, enclosing us in a smaller and smaller circle.

"I was in many battles, but the main thing they used me for in the Old City was repairing guns. I had no instruments, no lathe, no shaper. But I saved many machine guns. I even repaired a Lewis gun. It wasn't a particularly good weapon, but it had great psychological effect because it made a very loud noise when you shot it. I also had a grenade factory. We made bombs out of tin cans. I used to break windows in order to put the glass particles inside them. Whenever we got hold of some gunpowder we made grenades.

"When we surrendered we were told that, according to the terms of the negotiations, all fighters would go to prison camp and all civilians, doctors and wounded would be allowed to go into the New City. At one point I saw Dr. Riss take off his white coat. A fellow picked it up, put it on, said to the Arabs, 'I'm a doctor,' and escaped.

"There was another fellow who said to me, 'Let's dress like civilians and get out of here.' I was unshaven. With my red beard I looked like a gangster. 'No,' I said. 'I'm going with the other fellows to prison.' Well, he took two children by the hand, and when an Arab officer asked him whose children they were he said, 'They're mine.'

"'Where's their mother?' the officer asked.

"'She was killed,' he answered, walking on. They weren't his children at all. But he got away with it, while I went to prison.

"That same evening I helped carry the wounded to the Armenian hospital on my back. Arab terrorists tried to kill us. The Arab Legion stepped in and shot at least two of them. As I was carrying the wounded past Zion Gate, the Jews started shooting from outside the walls. Soon there was a heavy exchange of gunfire between the Arabs and the Jews. The Arabs

were afraid the Jews were trying to break in again. "Now, there were a thousand refugees in the Old City, and they were held up by all this shooting. Nisan Zeldes went with a white flag to order the Jews to stop shooting. He took off his undershirt and started shouting 'Don't shoot! Don't shoot!'

"An Arab sergeant stopped him and asked, 'If I let you go out of the Old City, will you come back?' Zeldes said he would.

"On Mount Zion he told an Israeli officer he had to go back because he'd given the Arabs his word. Zeldes was unable to get back into the Jewish Quarter that night because of a curfew. In the morning he came back. This fellow restored my faith in humanity.

"At the time we surrendered I didn't believe the Arabs would take us to prison camp. I was born here, so I know them. It's not that I was afraid. I just don't trust them. I had a revolver with me, and said to myself, 'If they try to kill me it will cost them dearly.' I had hidden my revolver in a loaf of bread. When the Arabs searched me I pretended to eat the bread. This fooled them. They never found my gun. I thought I was pretty smart. But when I got to camp, I found I was not the only one who managed to bring in a weapon. One fellow from another group of prisoners managed to sneak in a tommy gun. He strapped it to his leg and wrapped bandages around it. All in all, we managed to bring in some thirty or forty weapons. The Arabs never found them.

"While in camp, Zeldes and I became good friends. I was not well educated, having only finished elementary school, but I did like mathematics. Zeldes taught me algebra, geometry and trigonometry.

"As I was a mechanic, the British sometimes sent me to work outside the camp. They didn't have to urge me. I used to repair the water pumps at the military camps. At one camp I met a British officer. He asked me if I knew about gardening. As it happens, I don't know a thing about it, but I told him I did. I took three fellows who didn't know any more about gardening than I did along with me. For eight months we were the gardeners for several British officers. We'd go to one of the gardens, give two or three cigarettes to the Arab soldier guarding us, then settle down to listen to the radio. After eight months of this sort of gardening, we didn't have one flower to show for it.

"In camp we slept on the ground. It was very cold at night. I gathered newspapers, brought them back to the camp, and made mattresses out of them to provide insulation against the cold ground. Noticing that Zeldes was coughing, I made him a mattress like mine and said to him, 'You're sick. Take it.' One day when I went over to his tent I saw he didn't have the mattress. 'Where is it?' I asked.

"'There are old people here,' Zeldes said. 'One is eighty. He needed it more than I do.' He'd given it away to an old man. Zeldes certainly gave you faith in people. He was a kind of symbol for me.

"When the time came to leave prison camp, everyone hoped to be the first to leave. Zeldes was entitled to go out first. He was wounded and he'd received a message that his father had been killed fighting at Abu Ghosh. 'You must go,' I told him.

"'No. I'm young,' Zeldes said. 'I'll go last.'

"And that he did, closing the door behind him.

"When I got back from prison camp everybody had suggestions for me. They wanted me to become a police officer, go into the army, or work with my father. At the time my father already had a partner. I don't like anybody giving me orders, so I said I wanted to work on my own. But the partner left, and I began working with my father. It must have been 1951 when I went into partnership with him. He was an old man—afraid to think big. We didn't get enough work to eat. I started with no money at all. Now I could sell this business for three million pounds.

"I have a workshop and rent out a restaurant. I like to work. Once I had a company that produced record players, among other things. But now it's very difficult to find good workers in Israel. Good Jewish workers are drafted into the army. If you ask for workers to replace them, they send you Arabs. We have a government bureau here and I have to telephone them if I need someone. I can't hire a worker off the street. But the bureau can send me whoever they like. 'Give me Jews,' I always say. But Israeli Jews are not workers anymore, either. Every father wants his son to be a doctor, a professor, an engineer. Simple workers are very hard to find.

"At Pinchas Oestreicher & Partners, Ltd., my partners are my wife and daughter. We do all sorts of repairs on lathes and welding machines. Five people work for me now, but I could give work to five hundred. There's enough work here. But the taxes are very high. I'm satisfied with what I have. I don't want to grow too big and get involved with higher taxes."

Mrs. Miriam Levy, like most housewives of the Jewish Quarter in the Old City, went around her house barefoot. Whenever the Arabs shelled the quarter during the siege, she would rush out of her home to Yochanan Ben Zakkai, the Sephardic synagogue then serving as a shelter. The quarter was shelled for the last time on the morning of the surrender. The distressed Mrs. Levy dashed out of the house barefoot, leaving her shoes and her seven-year-old daughter Rachel (page 162) behind. She didn't realize she would never again go back home.

After the surrender, Miriam Levy left the synagogue and headed toward Zion Gate. Caught up in the slow-moving crowd, she was close to the gate when shooting broke out between the Arabs and Israelis. The Arabs closed the gate and ordered the refugees to stay where they were. Miriam Levy and a group of about a hundred spent the night wondering if they would ever see the dawn. The next morning—Saturday, May 29—the shooting subsided. The group was allowed to proceed through Zion Gate. Miriam found her daughter Rachel, her husband Daniel, and their son Sasoon in the New City. Only then did she realize she had no shoes on and that her feet were bleeding.

Zidkyahu Michaeli lives in Ashdod on the Mediterranean. He belongs to a trucking cooperative.

On the day the mandate ended and the British withdrew from the New City, Michaeli was sent in with a Haganah force. Poking around the offices of the deserted British compound, he came upon two electric calculating machines that had been left behind. He took them to a store to have them appraised. The store was about to close for lunch. The owner told Michaeli to leave the machines and come back at three o'clock.

Michaeli then ran into a group of friends who were setting out on an operation. He decided to join them and was sent into the Old City as one of its defenders. "Two days before we surrendered," Michaeli told me, "the situation was desperate. I knew it was only a question of time. We didn't have any ammunition. I was told to use the Bren gun, one shot at a time. There wasn't any choice but to surrender. I told my friend Moshe Hasson (page 150) that perhaps we should try to escape by throwing ropes over the Old City wall. But we didn't have time. Hasson suggested we change into civilian clothes. I told him to remain in uniform, because we'd be better treated. I had once read in a Japanese book that soldiers hold each other in esteem.

"After the surrender we were collected together in one of the squares. I remember Major Tel standing there with a swagger stick under his arm saying, 'All fighters go to the left. All others remain where they are.' About eighteen or twenty of us moved to where Tel was pointing. We were sent to prison camp.

"About a month after my release I went back to the store where I'd left my two calculating machines. The owner said he was very happy I hadn't been killed and gave me eighty pounds."

"I was born in Hebron, Judea, in 1924 and survived the 1929 pogrom there," Moshe Hasson, a judge in Jerusalem's magistrate court, related. "Arabs broke into my father's house. My older sister and I were hiding behind some bookshelves. One Arab carrying a sword found us. I can still remember him telling my sister, 'Give me the money or I'll kill you!' My sister ran into my father's cloth shop, which was in our house, and found it had been looted and everything had been stolen. The Arab was very angry. Fortunately a Moslem friend of my father's arrived and took us with him. Seventy people were massacred that day. It was the end of the Jewish community in Hebron. We settled in Jerusalem and my father started all over again.

"For a Jew everything starts in Jerusalem. The Old City is the heart of the nation. That's why we defended the Jewish Quarter in 1948. I was among those sent in to fight there. We were picked at random. I didn't have to think about the reasons I was defending the Jewish Quarter. Those thoughts come into your head when you volunteer. And you volunteer because you want to fight for your people. I know that among us there were those who gave some thought to the meaning of Jerusalem, the Holy City. But I just fought for my life and the lives of those in the quarter. I'll venture to say that no one can fight and think at the same time.

"On our way to POW camp," Judge Hasson went on to say, "the legion exhibited us at all the Palestinian refugee camps in Jordan to prove that the Arabs had been victorious. At one of these camps I looked out of the bus window and recognized an Arab I knew. His name was Hamad Karaini. He had been a messenger at the Immigration Department where I worked before the war. 'I don't want to see Hamad,' I said to myself. I put a hand over my face, hoping that the bus would move on. Unfortunately, Hamad got on the bus and saw me. Our eyes met.

"'Oh! Mr. Hasson,' Hamad said. 'You are a member of the Haganah!'

"I didn't answer. He came closer and spat in my face."

Leah Wultz and her husband Yechiel strolled past the building that was once their old school. Leah had been a teacher there, and Yechiel, the headmaster. It would have surprised the two young Israeli soldiers who overtook them on Batei Mahse Street that this quiet, retired couple had once manufactured bombs. Leah learned to make bombs after she joined the Irgun Zvei Leumi, a terrorist organization that was fighting British rule in the last years of the Palestine mandate. Caught by the British, the attractive young firebrand served two years in a Bethlehem jail.

"When I got out," Leah recalled as we sat in her living room, "I had to report every day to the police station. Irgun sent me into the Old City to organize the underground there and teach school, but one of the British counterintelligence officers recognized me. He tried to prevent me from entering. It was only after I showed him documents from the Department of Education, which proved I was a bonafide schoolteacher, that he reluctantly let me go into the Old City."

With her experience in making bombs and hand grenades, Leah operated the Jewish Quarter's munitions plant during the siege. The plant reached a production peak of one hundred bombs a day. The only real skill required was in making the fuse.

"Setting an electric detonator was very delicate and dangerous work," Leah told me. "You had to tie five matches around the detonator, which a fighter then struck before throwing. We recommended he count to three, because, if he threw it too soon, the Arabs had time to toss it right back. The best bombs were made from Player's tin cigarette boxes filled with powder, bits of glass, or nuts and bolts. I picked Yechiel to make the fuses because he had the hands of a virtuoso, having been a passionate cello player for fifteen years."

At the time of the surrender these two found themselves conscience stricken. After much soul searching, Leah and Yechiel decided there was only one course to follow. "I'll tell you a secret," Leah said as she poured me a cup of coffee. "Yechiel was supposed to be evacuated with the civilians. He was to go out as a doctor. In fact he was already dressed like one, having borrowed a long white coat from the hospital. But then we sat down and talked it over. Yechiel, as headmaster, had a responsibility to the teachers and pupils of his school. I said, 'Yechiel, you can't leave and let them stay.' So he took off the white coat and went to the prison camp with the others.

"I was evacuated through Zion Gate to the New City and went straight home. 'What's happened?' my parents asked. I began to cry. 'We've lost the Old City,' I said, 'and Yechiel has gone to prison.'"

Joseph Dahan, a Sabra and government employee, is known to friends as Skip, a nickname he acquired at the age of twelve while in the Jewish Youth Movement. One day he went to the movies with some friends. The picture was *Skipper of the Sea*. Dahan's friends did not speak English and puzzled over the title, wondering if they wanted to go in. Dahan, who had learned English at a Catholic school, convinced them it was a good adventure film by translating the title. "So you speak English, 'Skip,'" one of the boys said, and Skip he was thereafter. Like most nicknames, Skip fits Dahan's colorful personality.

"I can't recall when we went into the Jewish Quarter," Dahan said as he reclined in an armchair on the balcony of his Jerusalem apartment. A partial invalid as the result of a war wound, he still perks up at recollection of the siege. "But I know the British were still around. And how! Four of us were sent into the quarter illegally in a British Bren carrier. We were trying to reinforce the Jewish Quarter before the mandate ended, and the British did all they could to stop us. But the Haganah managed to get in touch with some British army personnel and made arrangements for us to be smuggled in.

"We were to go into the Old City through Jaffa Gate, where the Arab irregulars had set up a barricade. We had no weapons, because it was against the Haganah regulations to carry arms. I said to my superior officer, 'I'm not going into the Old City till I've got a weapon.' I said that because a day or so earlier the driver of a Bren carrier had turned four boys over to the Arabs. They'd been slaughtered in cold blood.

"'You're a troublemaker,' my officer said.

"'Yes, I am a troublemaker,' I said, 'I don't want to get killed. Give me some kind of weapon so if I die, I die fighting.' He brought me a bayonet.

"As we approached Jaffa Gate in the Bren carrier, the driver turned off the wireless light. We passed the barricade and were surrounded by Arabs. The driver stopped the Bren carrier and, leaving the hatch open as if there was nothing amiss, got out and walked over to an Arab shop. 'Look,' I said to the Englishman before he got out, 'I'm a kid, so I don't know what fear is. If you pull anything, God help you.'

"The Arabs looked down into the open hatch. I said to myself, 'God bless this bayonet.' It was dark inside, so they didn't see us. Five minutes later the English soldier came back, casually eating a sandwich. He had done this to make it look as though nothing was going on.

"We drove past the *kishleh* prison and stopped at the Armenian Quarter. We slipped into Rehov Ha Yehudim, where Rusnak was waiting for us, as he knew additional forces were being sent in. I think we managed to smuggle eight fighters into the old Jewish Quarter that way."

During the fighting Skip Dahan exchanged his bayonet for a Finnish tommy gun. "The Tommy Finni has a bigger calibre than the Thompson," Dahan beamed. "It has a round magazine with seventy-two bullets. It's wonderful for house-to-house fighting. With that gun no one could touch you. We had two Tommy Finnis in the Old City. I had one of them because I was in the tactical reserve. We'd get calls all the time: 'Please send help. The Arabs are here . . . the Arabs are there . . .' So we'd go here, we'd go there, to repel the attacks.

"Defending the Jewish Quarter was my personal fight. I had been to school there. And as we were very poor, my grandfather wanted me to have a good education. He sent me to a free Catholic school. We were only twelve Jews out of 360 boys. That is why I know two languages and two ways of life—the Arab and the Jewish. But the Arabs at school made me feel like a worthless old rag—a *shmatteh*. I was always getting into fights and only managed to uphold my honor when I finally got them to say to me, 'Good morning, Mr. Joseph.'

"When I fought in the Old City, I felt I was a part of this land. This land was mine. It belonged to me. I wanted to liberate everything and be a free man, not a worthless old rag.

"After seven days of fighting I collapsed. They thought I was dead. My skin was yellow. Masha Weingarten gave me ether to drink. She told me, 'After half an hour you'll feel like a bull. You'll revive, and want to go on.' And I did feel exactly like a bull. I continued fighting another seven days. What kept me going was the ether. I felt great.

"When I got to the POW camp after the surrender I slept for two days."

Penina Even Tov looked over the shoulder of her son, Chen, to check his homework. A schoolteacher today in Tel Aviv, Penina was her son's age—fourteen—when she was evacuated from the Jewish Quarter in 1948. Seated in the living room of her apartment, she reminisced about the Old City, where she was born and brought up.

"Our house was very close to the Wailing Wall," Penina recalled. "From our windows we could see everyone who went past. There was a barricade and I can remember watching the British soldiers search people as they came to pray at the wall. We watched everything that went on. We lived it."

Penina paused and studied the picture I had taken of her during the evacuation at Zion Gate, where she is seen turning back and calling out to her mother. "I was filled with hatred for the Arabs," Penina said.

"One brother had been killed on May 16, the other was taken prisoner with my father on May 28. As I looked around the crowd I saw my sister crying and heard my three-year-old nephew say to her, 'Why do you cry? Believe in God and everything will be all right.'

"Behind me my mother, a small woman, was struggling vainly with a large bundle in her arms. 'Put it down! Put it down!' I shouted. 'You'll fall and get trampled.' I wanted to carry the bundle but couldn't get back to her in the crowd. An Arab soldier shouted to me that everything would be all right and helped load the bundle on my mother's head. Imagine her courage! She told the Arab, 'This time it's the Jews who have to leave the Old City. Next time it'll be your turn.'

"After the liberation of the Jewish Quarter in 1967, my mother came to see me. 'You see, I was right,' she said."

Yaacov Ben Rubi is a director of the Masad Bank in Jerusalem. He belonged to the original garrison that defended the Old City and was a member of the Irgun, considered a terrorist organization in its day. Asked about his feelings when the Jewish Quarter was liberated, Ben Rubi said, "I cried."

When Malca Shimoni Dash, a schoolteacher, was evacuated from the Jewish Quarter late one night after the surrender, she carried with her a variety of messages to people in the New City. The dominant thought in everyone's mind at the time was the question of how to get some word back home. Each captive wanted to reassure his family that he was safe and well, even though he might be on his way to POW camp in Jordan. Preparing meaningful messages for clandestine delivery without attracting the Arabs' attention required the utmost ingenuity. The style and content of these messages varied as much as the personalities of the senders.

"The most reliable couriers were nurses and school-teachers, because they knew everybody," Mrs. Dash told me the afternoon she and her husband visited an open-air exhibit called "The Forest" by the Israeli sculptor Menashe Kadishman at Jerusalem's Israel Museum. Among these no one was more sought after as a message-bearer than Malca, for she had doubled as a soldier at night and had also got to know most of the fighters in the Old City. So when Malca passed through Zion Gate and reached the Israeli lines at midnight, she carried with her an interesting assortment of messages.

One unusual message came from Mordechai Pinkas (page 170), who was to remain in the army. To notify his father that he was alive and safe, Pinkas simply sent his Webley pistol.

The most dramatic communiqué, however, was transmitted by Malca unexpectedly, by word of mouth, at three in the morning as she rode in an army truck filled with refugees on the road to Jerusalem. At one point, when the convoy pulled up for a brief halt, she heard a voice call out, "Tell me, tell me ... is my son Nisan Zeldes alive?"

"I recognized the voice of my uncle," she said, "and as I'd seen my cousin shortly before, acting as a UN interpreter at Zion Gate, I shouted out as the truck started up, 'If you want to see your son, go up to Mount Zion. He's with the UN delegate helping the wounded.'

"I saw my uncle a few days later and he told me he had found his son, kissed him, and talked with him till morning, then watched him go back through Zion Gate into the Old City, because he had given his word to an Arab he would do so. Nisan would not take advantage of being in Israeli-held territory, so he returned and went to POW camp. His father didn't encourage him to break his word, because he himself was in the army, and a man of honor. My cousin Nisan was in POW camp for eleven months. I'm glad Nisan had a chance to see him, because his father was killed two weeks later in the fighting at Abu Ghosh."

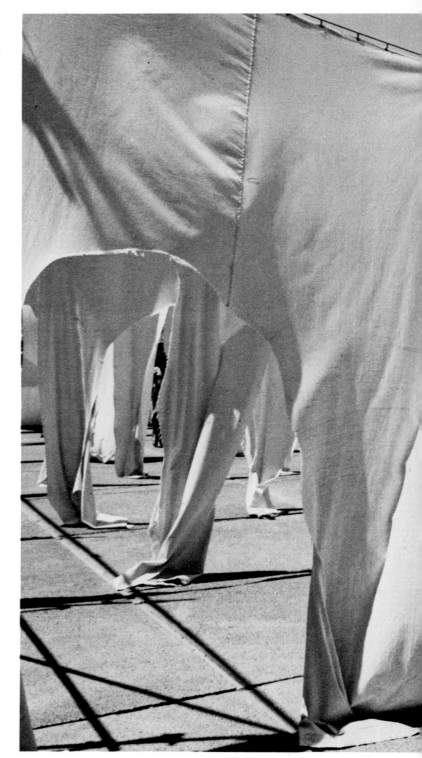

Rachel Ma'atuk Levy is the wife of a Jerusalem taxi driver. Nobody would recognize in this cheerful housewife the terrified little girl who ran down the flaming Street of the Jews in 1948. This is how Rachel recalls that ordeal.

"I was seven and a half years old at the time. I had been left at home, because my mother had gone to the synagogue with the other children and had forgotten me in the general confusion. So I took some matzohs, which were on the table, and went out. There were Arab soldiers in the street, and the quarter was burning. I had no choice but to run through the streets trying to find my parents. I got to Zion Gate and was pushed through by the crowd. An Israeli soldier on the other side put me on a truck with other refugees. He wanted to take my matzohs away from me because there was so little room in the truck. But I hung onto them. The next day I found my mother (page 146), my father and my little brother Sasoon. I gave my mother the matzohs. She divided them among us, because there was nothing else to eat. We were taken to a huge house with many rooms. It was three stories high. My only fear during all this time was climbing those stairs and not being able to get down again. I wasn't used to houses like that. I'd never seen stairs before."

162

Israel Katzburg threw a homemade grenade at an Arab Legion soldier in door-to-door fighting during the siege. The Arab threw it back, wounding him in the leg. Once again Israel Katzburg had survived and works today as the registrar of the Bar-Ilan University in Tel Aviv.

The Katzburgs were the last family to get out of Czechoslovakia officially before the war broke out. The father owned a wholesale chocolate business in Bratislava and employed forty. "Until the Nazis came," Katzburg sighed as we sat in his Tel Aviv living room, "Czechoslovakia was really a paradise. I don't think the Jews had a better life anywhere. It was a real democracy. Then came Munich.

"'Aryanization' started at that time. Aryans took over Jewish businesses for a nominal sum of money. My father realized it was the end of Czechoslovakia and decided to emigrate to Palestine. It took him several months to get the necessary papers and the money transferred officially; I believe it was a thousand pounds. Then Hitler marched into Prague. When my father went there to make arrangements for our departure he was beaten up.

"Bratislava had between fifteen and twenty thousand Jews. Most were taken to Auschwitz in 1944. The curious thing is that not many Jews left Bratislava of their own free will. I even had relatives who left Palestine and went back to Czechoslovakia in 1939, after the war broke out. Conditions weren't rosy here. They thought they'd survive the war and everything would be as before. They really didn't grasp the situation and just couldn't believe . . ."

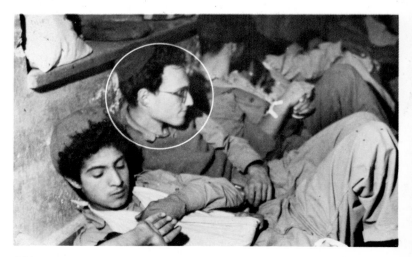

Moshe Yabrov works for the Leumi Bank in Jerusalem. He was born in Poland and emigrated to Palestine in 1939. At that time the Jewish population totaled around 300,000. Eight years later—when Yabrov was a member of the unit sent in to relieve the Jewish Quarter—the number had doubled.

"When we broke into the Old City," Yabrov said, "the people there had enough food and water. What they needed was the ammunition we brought in. Of course, it wasn't enough because of the overwhelming number of Arabs we were fighting. Until our arrival the Arab irregulars had been besieging the quarter. But after the breakthrough the legion entered the fight. They put in two companies to tip the balance in favor of surrender. We knew we could expect no mercy from the irregulars. We hoped it would be different with the legion.

"After we surrendered my most vivid recollection is of an Arab Legion officer saying to us, 'From this moment on you are prisoners of King Abdullah and cannot be touched.' That meant the Arab irregulars and civilians couldn't harm us. And that was a piece of luck."

Ora Dagan Napacha, one of the three nurses in the Jewish Quarter during the siege, now lives with her husband on a *kibbutz* near Haifa. There she recalled her experiences during the siege.

"I took the nursing course at Hadassah hospital. Then I was asked if I wanted to go into the Old City. I agreed because I was eager to get the experience and thought I would be more useful there.

"I entered the Old City in the beginning of May 1948, just before the British mandate ended. Each month the doctors and nurses there were relieved on a rotation system. The British sent in two convoys a week, both on the same day. I wanted to enter on the first convoy to have enough time to be briefed by the nurse I was relieving before she left on the second convoy. The British didn't allow it, because they were afraid we would both remain in the Old City.

"Hadassah kept three doctors there, along with an operating room nurse, a social nurse and an orderly. I was a social nurse. I worked with children and pregnant women. When the battle began on the fourteenth of May, Masha (page 88) and I worked day and night in surgery with the rest of the medical team. Masha dealt with the dying. I didn't have the heart for it.

"When Yitzhak Mizrachi died I knew it was the end. In terrible situations you tend to believe in predestination. Yitzhak had been wounded before, and always recovered. He would leave us, go back to fight, and then return with another wound. The last time he was brought in we doctors and nurses knew it was the end. And it turned out to be true. He died on the last day of the siege.

"The day after we surrendered, the serious cases were sent to the New City. Our medical team was the last to leave. It was not yet dark when we went through Zion Gate. There was a little road between the gate and the walls of the Dormition church on Mount Zion. We remained there until the moon went down, then proceeded to the New City.

"I was in shock when we got there. For two months all I did was sleep and go every day to visit the wounded. My friends wanted to take me to dinner parties, but I didn't want to see anybody. I could not speak to anyone who had not been with us in Jerusalem."

Of all the fighters who defended the Jewish Quarter, only Mordechai Pinkas elected to stay in the army, first activated in 1921 under the name Haganah, meaning "defense." At forty-nine, he is one of the oldest active officers in the Israeli army.

By the time Pinkas, a Sabra born in Jerusalem, joined the Haganah it had become an illegal army. In 1946 he trained recruits, and early in 1948 was assigned to the Jewish Quarter. The quarter was then divided into two commands, each with six posts, every post manned by half-a-dozen boys and a girl or two. This was the nucleus of the Jewish Quarter's garrison when the War of Independence broke out. Leaning against a low wall in Batei Mahse, Colonel Pinkas gazed affectionately at two children on a slide. Pointing to the playground he said, "There used to be a well here, where we hid some of our weapons after we surrendered."

He went on to reminisce about that fateful day. "Until noon the question was whether or not to surrender. We realized we couldn't do anything more and decided that our duty was to save the lives of the civilians. A meeting was held and we called together the commanders, a doctor, and Benshemesh, a private. Everyone spoke his mind. The vote was unanimous for surrender. There was only one abstention.

"When the Arabs came through our lines I had the feeling I wasn't really there, that it wasn't really happening to me. Somehow I was outside myself, looking down on myself. It was a very curious sensation, as if you were split in two—your body itself, and your vision of yourself. This feeling lasted until nightfall."

As Colonel Pinkas and I left Batei Mahse, he took one last look around and said, "With the weapons we had then you couldn't even start a small South American revolution today. But the emotions and ideals matched those of World War II. There was no comparison between the enormous importance of the conflict and the small calibre of the weapons."

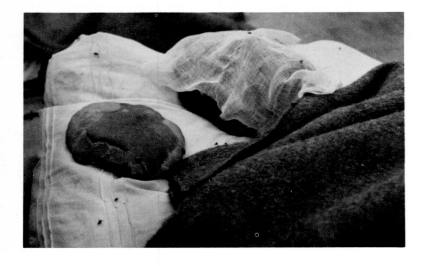

Moshe Mishale, now a clerk at Jerusalem's city hall, took a burst of Bren gun fire in the right jaw two days before the surrender.

"I was wounded in the afternoon," Mishale, a native of the Jewish Quarter, remembers. "I must have looked like a slaughtered cow, because they put me in the morgue. During the night someone came in to leave a body and heard me tapping on the floor. Dr. Riss was called in. 'Moshe's alive!' he said. 'Take him to the operating room.'

"I'd swallowed my tongue. He got it out with a pair of forceps. Dr. Riss told me an operation would be very risky. I couldn't speak. They gave me a piece of paper and a pencil. I wrote 'I trust you.'

"Dr. Riss smiled, and I felt better. In the middle of the operation the lights went out. They had to finish with flashlights fastened to their heads.

"I was lying in Batei Mahse after the operation when I saw soldiers outside. 'What's going on?' I wrote on a scrap of paper. 'It's finished,' someone told me. 'We've surrendered.'

"A Red Cross doctor and an Arab doctor came by. 'This one is almost dead,' the Arab doctor said. 'You can take him. He's not coming with us.'

"My head was bandaged and I was barefoot. I was being helped from Zion Gate to an ambulance when I stumbled and rolled all the way down the steep hill to the wadi.

"I was in Hadassah hospital for a year and a half on a liquid diet—milk, milk, milk. My jaw was shattered. There were eight operations. They took a bone from here and a bone from there. A specialist from South Africa operated on me. Then a Canadian surgeon performed two more operations. I still go to Hadassah every week. They are trying to strengthen the muscles of my jaw. To this day I can only eat mashed potatoes and liquids.

"When I left the hospital I went to work as a taxi driver. It wasn't good for me. You don't have time to eat regularly. One day it's breakfast at nine, another time lunch at three. The doctors said I must eat at regular hours. Now I work with the municipality of Jerusalem. I have a very nice home, a beautiful wife, and five lovely children. Every Friday I go to the Wailing Wall to pray. I'm a happy man, even when I don't feel so good. It's better than being dead."

Chaim Alcotzer is six years younger than his brother Meir (page 74). Like his brother, Chaim was born in the Jewish Quarter. He lived there until the surrender in 1948. Today Chaim's one ambition is to move from the New City back to the old quarter.

Chaim was sixteen years old during the siege. While he was covering the retreat of the men from his post, he was severely wounded in the left leg. His worst moment came when he was informed that, in spite of his youth and the gravity of his wound, he was being sent from Jerusalem to a Jordanian POW camp. At the camp an Arab doctor told Chaim he planned to amputate his leg at the knee to prevent gangrene. "I'd rather die with both feet than live with only one," Chaim protested vehemently. A British doctor then examined Chaim and advised him he had to cut off the foot at the ankle. Again Chaim demurred. No amputation was performed. He hobbled around the camp until he was released and sent back to Jerusalem. After two operations there, he was left with a slight limp.

Chaim first went to work as a driver for the Ministry of Agriculture before transferring to the Israel Government Tourist Office. Now he organizes tours around the country for visiting dignitaries. In 1967, shortly before the Six Day War, he confided to a friend, "If I was offered a trip anywhere in the world, the place I'd like to go is around the corner to the Jewish Quarter."

In 1971 Chaim's life ambition seemed close to fulfillment. He succeeded in buying a three-room apartment on Lahaim Street, just off the Street of the Jews. "It's completely furnished and ready for immediate occupancy," Chaim told me, "but my wife Sima refuses to move to the Jewish Quarter. She's afraid that if we live there she will feel isolated."

Professor Leonard Binder, director of the Center for Middle East Studies at the University of Chicago, was born in 1927. His Russian immigrant father was "the usual thing in the Boston needle trade—a small-time manufacturer of women's clothing." Binder's curriculum vitae is a prototype of the gifted academic. He took his bachelor's degree at Harvard in 1952, then spent one year at Princeton and another at Oxford. He worked on his doctoral dissertation in Pakistan and won his Ph.D. in Middle East studies and political science at Harvard in 1955. That fall he began teaching at UCLA. He did field research in Iran and Egypt before going to the University of Chicago in 1961 where he has since remained, except for excursions to Lebanon and Tunisia. When I looked into the classroom where Leonard Binder was lecturing I could see little resemblance between this dignified professor with neatly trimmed beard and the young fighter I had photographed in 1948. "Remember, I was born in Boston, and the Arab world came across to me in a different way than it did to the Jews of Palestine," Professor Binder observed as we sat in his office overlooking the campus. "Visiting Palestine in 1947 with my wife Yona seemed like a good idea, not only because I had been engaged in the youth activities of Boston's Jewish community, but because I was very much interested in getting a good university education. You see, I hadn't done very well in high school, so my college prospects weren't too good here. Going to Jerusalem looked as though it might be rewarding in a number of ways. "We had only been in Jerusalem two months and I hadn't really got my feet on the ground yet, intellectually speaking, when all hell broke loose with the announcement of Partition on November 29. We were at a small hotel and all the kids staying there went out to celebrate. Yona and I didn't go. We were not yet attuned to how important an occasion it was. The next day we sort of understood a little better. Already there were stones being thrown and shops set on fire, and there was some risk of disorder. From that day on it was impossible to concentrate on studies. We students were collected together a couple of days at a time and shown how to shoot a gun and what to do with a hand grenade.

"In February of 1948 I was with a part-time unit organized in such a way that we had two weeks on duty and two weeks off. While the science students studied, the humanities students pulled military duty, then the reverse. Yona was a science student, while I was in the humanities. Let's say it made things a bit of a problem. Then I got into a local defense unit.

"I had made arrangements to see Yona on May 17, but had to cancel them because my platoon got called out and sent to Yemin Moshe, where we joined a group of around eighty. From there Gazit led us up to Mount Zion. We climbed the hill leading to the mount after dark, carrying heavy mortar shells for the Davidka—you know, that crazy homemade super-mor-

tar. That night on the mount I saw members of the Palmach lined up near the outer wall of the Old City. They were young kids, exhausted and bandaged. "They started the breakthrough of Zion Gate by firing the Davidka. The trajectory of the first shell was short. Instead of falling inside the Old City, where the Arabs manned the walls, it fell on our side. There was a great outpouring of black smoke and sparks that went up maybe a hundred feet in the air. I just gasped. A guy who was a little closer than I began to scream, 'You're crazy! You're hitting us!' The second shell went over the wall. It didn't do very much damage, but it did scare away the Arabs defending the wall. A group of engineers went up and planted a charge on the iron gate. The gate came crashing down and the Palmach went in. There was some fighting in the immediate vicinity before contact was made with the Jewish Quarter.

"At daybreak our group was assembled and we went in. We weren't told very much of anything. The night before, we had been briefed on how we were to go through the Jewish Quarter and come out at Jaffa Gate. In other words, we were going to take the Old City. Well, we didn't have the men for that. All we did was slip into the Old City by filing along the wall up to the Armenian Quarter, where we were confronted with a wide open space under Arab fire. Each one of us in turn had to run across it as fast as he could, tumble into a sand lot, and roll down to the basement window of a matzoh factory, where two men reached out of the window and pulled him in. The Arabs firing at us from the Armenian monastery were using tracers. Fortunately, you could see where the fire was directed. If they had picked out one spot and concentrated on it, they would have got quite a few of us. As it was, they didn't get anybody."

At noon Binder took me to lunch in the campus cafeteria. He reminisced about street fighting in the Jewish Quarter and his time in the prison camp, and how these experiences had affected his life.

"After the fighting began, I was pretty scared a good bit of the time. First of all, it wasn't my kind of thing, you know, and then, it was not an anonymous form of fighting, such as you find in big wars, with shelling from great distances. We had to get up really close if we were going to kill the enemy. We were usually looking him right in the eye. It was a pretty horrible business—nasty, dirty, crude and terribly inefficient. At least very few people got killed, relatively speaking for a modern war. But it was damned frightening. The worst was that we were getting hit by mortars and twenty-five pounders all the time. I can recall how Michaeli (page 148) and another fellow were on a fortified balcony. They got a direct hit from an armored car, which took down the balcony and the sandbags and everything. They landed in a heap of sand on the first floor—boom! Luckily, they weren't hurt and were able to scramble out of the way. "The Arabs had heavy machine guns and mortars.

They even had armored cars. Some got through the narrow streets of the Old City and shot at us point blank. We had nothing—a couple of stolen Bren guns, a few Sten guns, and some old Enfield rifles. "I didn't do very much and don't recall hitting anybody. I can't recall being scared during the actual fighting either. You're all right in the heat of battle, when you've got to have your wits about you. The most difficult part is afterwards, when you are thinking about it, waiting for it to happen again, and don't know when it's going to come. That's when you get scared and say: 'Gee whiz! I'm only twenty years old.' "When there wasn't much fighting we'd walk around the streets in search of material to fortify the windows of our post. We tried to pick up some plants the civilians were growing in big gasoline cans. The women got very excited and began to shout at us. We had to shout back that it was for the defense of the quarter. Here we were, just about giving up the ghost, and these women were still trying to hang onto their potted plants.

"After the surrender we were taken prisoner and led off to the *kishleh*, the old Turkish prison in the Arab Quarter. Some newsmen in Arab headdress asked if there were any Americans among us. I was torn between the idea of saying 'Yes'—you know, sensational story in the newspapers . . . everybody will know I'm here . . . my family will know I'm alive . . . the publicity will safeguard my life—as opposed to the other possibility: some son of a bitch saying, 'There's an American. Let's get the bastard!' I stood there with my back to the bars of the cell. One of the prisoners said, 'What do you think, Lenny? Why don't you tell them?' I said, 'Forget it.' "We were exhausted, emotionally drained, glad to be alive. I expected, you know, that it was going to end in a holocaust. It was not a bloodbath or anything like that, so I was relieved about that. But I had a feeling of enormous letdown, of having no will, which is typical when you're taken prisoner, I think. "I was also depressed about the loss of the Jewish Quarter. But it would have meant much more to me if I'd had the chance to get acquainted with the quarter. From the time I arrived in Jerusalem, it was forbidden to enter the Old City. It was dangerous. I never even got within sight of the Wailing Wall. All I knew of the Jewish Quarter was what little I saw after we went through Zion Gate. I got as far as the police station on Rehov Hayehudim. "The first time I saw Batei Mahse was after we surrendered. Intellectually, I knew this was a great loss, but emotionally I only felt the enormity of it later on. It was only after I went to POW camp that I could put it all into a political and historical context. Then the significance of Jerusalem and my attachment to the city—both Old and New—became very, very strong. "On our last day in the Old City I wrote my wife a letter. In it I told her: 'I don't think we are going to survive . . . I think we are going to be killed, and if you ever get this letter, I just want you to know . . .' I sealed the letter and found an envelope with a cancelled stamp from the Old City of Jerusalem. The cancellation was on a National Jewish Fund stamp. I clearly recall what it said: JERUSALEM UNDER SIEGE. I gave the letter to a nurse, who was being evacuated, and asked her to drop it in a mailbox. It went through the mails and was delivered. When my wife got it she knew that, before the surrender at least, I was alive. I cherish this letter and the envelope with the stamp. It must be a collector's item by now. I'll give it to my grandchildren. It'll make them rich.

"At the Jordan POW camp in Mafraq we were divided into groups. Each tent slept ten. You got very close to the men in your tent. We had friends in the other tents, and we had enemies. People were arranged in categories. The religious groups from the Old City were allocated by ethnic origin. The Kurds all stayed together and so did the various Hassidic groups, the Sephardim and the Ashkenazi. We sorted ourselves out on the first day. The Arabs just gave us the material for setting up our tents.

"Soon after we got to the POW camp we had a bright sunny day. Everybody was enjoying the sun. It was so hot the religious people went around without their shirts on, but still wore the equivalent of prayer shawls they always keep on under their clothes. One of them—a particularly bent-over, thin fellow who had hardly ever seen the light of day because he was always at his Talmud studies—was wandering around aimlessly. He went up to a friend and said to him in Yiddish: 'Just think how bad it's going to be this winter.'
"Here it was a lovely summer day. We could breathe freely. No one was bothering us. And here was this old man worrying about next winter. This is the typical Jewish attitude. You think ahead to the worst. You have to force yourself not to enjoy the moment too much because it's going to get worse. You've got to start worrying about winter because it's going to be a bad one.

"One of the most important things at the prison camp was the organization of our own affairs. We had a representative system. The main thing was the distribution of food and the organization of accounts. We had our own military police to maintain order and do whatever cleaning had to be done—cooking, carrying water and so on.
"My own functions included the distribution of food and seeing to it there were no conflicts about the portions, for we didn't get enough to eat and were often hungry and upset. Some would crowd around and steal an extra helping. The food was very bad, beneath contempt, and far from nourishing. On top of that, if you had to fight for it, an unhealthy atmosphere was created.

"Tuval and some of the others negotiated with the Arabs and reached an agreement whereby we could organize ourselves. We got kosher and nonkosher food and distributed it to people accordingly. Actually, I had my first real lessons in social science living in the camp and observing the hierarchical structure and the differential distribution of goods.

"Whenever a truckload of food parcels from home was distributed the whole camp became electrified. We were all excited. If your name wasn't called, you were crestfallen. We all hoped to get letters from our families, although they weren't supposed to write. But there was usually something in the packages. Everything was wrapped in newspaper, so the Hebrew papers would reach us.
"One day my name was called out. I ran down and waited in line, and got a huge package of food and cigarettes like those sent to all the *mahalniks*—the volunteer fighters who came over especially to fight in the Israeli army. The package was from the Palestine Mortgage Bank. There were lots of cigarettes, terrible South African ones I couldn't smoke, and some good ones too. One was glad to get all the commodities, even if without the personal touch. Everybody in my tent was delighted to share in it though. For a while we were the richest tent in the camp.

"My wife wasn't sure when I'd get back from prison camp, because the names of those released were not given out ahead of time. The Jerusalemites knew beforehand when a group was arriving and could meet them, but my wife was staying in a village near Tel Aviv.
"The first day after my release I got as far as Sarafand, half way between Jerusalem and Tel Aviv. At the army camp there I was issued some clothes and told that the next morning a truck would deliver me wherever I wanted to go. But I just couldn't stand waiting and being left on my own. I got as far as Tel Aviv, and tried to get a bus to the village where my wife was living. But the last bus had left. I couldn't even call her up. She had no phone.
"The next morning, unceremoniously, I took the bus. It wasn't a very romantic way to return home. I was headed for the town of Even Yehuda, where my wife was staying with a family. They had guessed I might be coming, and were cooking something fancy for dinner. They weren't sure about the time I'd arrive or how I was traveling. The bus stopped about half a mile down the road. I didn't know where the house was, so I asked a kid. He ran ahead to announce my arrival.
"My wife knew I was coming about half a minute before I showed up. She was wearing an apron. It was a wonderful meeting, one of the great moments in my life. It wasn't like the homecomings in Jerusalem—the square jammed with people when the trucks arrived, entire families waiting to hug and kiss

the ones who returned, sheer bedlam.

"In my case it was far away, on a bright sunny day. There were just a few people around, and they kept their distance. A couple withdrew to the kitchen. Next door neighbors stood watching from the yard; people across the way watched from their front stoop. But no one came over at first. Yona and I had a few minutes to look at one another and realize the ordeal was over.

"For a while, after my return, I wasn't sure what I wanted to do. We were living now in Tel Aviv, and I started looking for jobs to find out what I could do. Nothing much turned up. I remember doing an art job for the Palestine Mortgage Bank—my benefactor when I was a prisoner. It was a poster showing the structure of the bank's industrial investments, which they were going to hang somewhere. It wasn't very good. I did a lousy job and, as far as I know, it was never used.

"Then I became a reporter for the Jewish Telegraph Agency. I hung out at the Public Information Office in a hotel we called the Ritz. It had a nice bar, a big lounge, and faced the Mediterranean. Three times a day I'd go down to the PIO, get whatever news was put out, and cable it to New York. I learned how to write cable-ese. Occasionally I would cover a story myself. Then I felt I was really in the big leagues. My salary was not large, but it wasn't too bad. Yona got a job teaching English in two schools. We rented a tiny room where we had to share kitchen and bathroom facilities—it was really beastly. And we paid an enormous sum for it. However, we managed to save some money on our combined salaries.

"In 1950 I decided that I wanted to go back to school in the States. I wanted to study politics—international relations, if possible. I wanted to learn about Middle Eastern affairs and more about the Arab countries. As I've said, the Arab world and the Arab style of life and their conflict with the Jews came across to me in a different way than it did to many Israelis. For me Israel and the Palestinian Jews represented new experiences and, on top of that, I was thrown into the Jewish Quarter before being sent off to a POW camp, where I had to submit to Arab authority. It became vitally important for me to understand what the Arabs were doing.

"I applied to Harvard College from Jerusalem, and took the College Board Examinations at the YMCA there. I was accepted. Yona and I left Israel early in June 1950. We spent a terrific week in Paris. A week in London was less exciting because we didn't have much money left. We went through everything before we got home. I started at Harvard in September and Yona went to Simmons College, where she majored in chemistry. We completed our degrees in 1952.

"I was in Chicago in 1967 when the Jewish Quarter was liberated during the Six Day War. There's no doubt that hearing the news was a great emotional experience. We had been there for ten days during the siege of 1948 waiting for help from the outside, realizing more and more that it wasn't going to come. Psychologically the walls had grown higher and higher and more impenetrable. Our situation had become more and more hopeless.

"Now all at once the walls were breached and Israeli forces got into the Old City and down to the Wailing Wall. The Jewish Quarter, which had been looted and burned and destroyed to a great extent, was restored to Jewish control. That was a very exciting thing, if only because it reminded us of all those hours we had spent in the Old City. There's hardly a moment that was not deeply impressed on my consciousness at the time—the hours of waiting, the hours of fighting, the hours of fleeing—all that together. The liberation of the Old City brought everything up to the surface. I just had to get back there and see it.

"On the first day I went with my wife and son to the wall. But already the religious people had gotten control. There were separate sections for men and women. I was quite upset by that. The idea that men and women ought to be separated is unacceptable to me.

"The next day I met Gazit. We went through Zion Gate and followed the route we had taken in 1948, down the Street of the Jews to the police station. There was an Arab cobbler in one of the little booths underneath the police station. I chatted with him in Arabic and asked his name, when he had arrived there, and where he had come from. I guess it made him a little nervous, which wasn't my intention.

"Then Gazit and I wandered down to Batei Mahse. I was trying very hard to remember everything, but I really hadn't seen much of the Old City. It seemed quite small. I felt somehow diminished because a very important thing in my life was so small.

"How do I feel about Israel?" Binder asked, repeating my question. "My particular experience, as I have told you, was out of the ordinary and I think it made for a profound change in my perspective. It probably influenced me toward a somewhat less parochial view of Israel and the Jewish people. Solving the Arab-Israeli problem will take hard work, intellectual effort and, besides that, a lot of good will. This, of course, requires a much better understanding on both sides. Unfortunately neither the Arabs nor the Israelis have invested nearly enough effort into creating a true cultural understanding of one another.

"A few people, situated as I have been—on the edge of both societies—can make some kind of contribution towards mutual understanding. It's not always an easy role, because you get criticized from both sides. One gets accused of all sorts of things. I am in a rather special situation in that I can't separate my experience in the siege of the Jewish Quarter from my professional role and my life commitment. Most of the people you've interviewed have had the same experience, but—and I don't mean this in a disparaging way—one is a baker, another is the owner of a machine shop, a third is a banker. For them the siege remains in the past. For me it's part of my daily life, something I can't forget or escape.

"Recently there was an article published in Beirut criticizing American scholarship on the Middle East as biased against the Arabs, and citing the fact that one of the leading people at one of the leading universities—myself—had actually fought for the Haganah and been a prisoner of war. They were asking how such a person could be objective. That's the context in which I live.

"My answer to this is: study the scholarly work and judge it on its own merit, not in terms of the author's background. I'm proud of all the things I've done. It's been a unique experience and I would not exchange it for anything in the world. While I'm not certain as to what all this may add up to in terms of my intellectual development, I do know that simple-minded characterizations on the nature of the Arab-Israeli problem just won't do. We've got to find a way of living together based on mutual understanding, mutual respect, and a mutual regard for the cultural integrity of each group. I do believe that I have a feeling of respect for all sides, along with an appreciation of the similarities and the differences between us. I also believe it requires not only dedicated study but a kind of psychological discipline to be able to put yourself in the other guy's shoes while not losing your own identity."

Joseph Almog was born in Jerusalem. Watching him on the day the Jewish Quarter surrendered, I realized how tough a Sabra could be. Of all the prisoners, only Almog stood at attention in the ragged line-up. Arms at the side, he looked straight ahead. He wore a military beret with nonchalance, and although his shirt and shorts were rumpled, Almog had that indefinable bearing which marks a professional soldier. When a British officer asked the prisoners if anyone had experience with explosives, it was Almog who answered for all of them: "Nobody."

"I said that," Almog recalled twenty-eight years later, "because I didn't know what might be expected of us. The British officer came up to me and asked, 'What do you think of the job we did on the Hurva synagogue?'

"'How much dynamite did you use to blow it up?' I asked.

"'A ton and a half,' he said.

"'With a ton and a half you could have blown up the whole Jewish Quarter,' I told him."

Joseph Almog volunteered to go into the Jewish Quarter after he heard that the Palmach was looking for men who knew their way around there. "I went along," he told me, "because my parents lived in the quarter."

He never got to see his sixteen-year-old sister. A fighter, she was killed the day before the breakthrough at Zion Gate. His kid brother was too young for the battle, but did fight in the Canal War. In the Six Day War he was a captain; in the Yom Kippur War, a major; and today, at thirty-three, he is a colonel.

Almog has fought in every one of his country's wars, and is presently in the reserve. What impressed me most as I listened to him was that, although he is hard-nosed, he feels no animosity toward the Arabs. "Fifty of them belong to my bus cooperative," Almog said. "Three were in the Arab Legion and fought against us in the Jewish Quarter. Now they invite me to their homes for coffee. We are going to live here all our lives, so we've got to get on with one another."

Daniel Levy is a serene eighty-two-year-old who lived the first fifty-three years of his life in the Jewish Quarter. According to his son Sasoon, a Jerusalem taxi driver, the secret of his father's good health is that nothing bothers the old gentleman.

This is not altogether true. Until he was seventy-five, Daniel Levy had a fruit stand at the Mahanei Yehuda open-air market in the New City. He was known for the delicious bananas he sold. The bananas were grown in Jericho. Old Mr. Levy got them from an Arab wholesaler who had a shop in the Old City. When the fighting broke out, Mr. Levy owed the Arab thirty pounds. But the Arab Quarter was cut off from the Jewish Quarter during the fighting and, after the 1948 war, the Old City was cut off from the New City. Having been incorporated into the Kingdom of Jordan, the Old City was inaccessible to Israelis. So Mr. Levy never got a chance to see the Arab wholesaler, pay his debt, or purchase any more bananas.

Nineteen years later, after the Six Day War, Daniel Levy was at last able to go back to the Old City, locate the wholesaler, pay up his debt and once again buy those delicious Jericho bananas.

Menahem Waxman, a lawyer in Haifa, immigrated from Poland in 1935 when he was eleven years old. In 1948, a law student, he went into the Jewish Quarter with the relief party. He has since participated in every one of Israel's wars. Waxman considers the Yom Kippur War of 1973 the toughest he went through, though on that occasion he was not in combat.

"I didn't have a very pleasant job in that war," Waxman said as we sat on the veranda of his Haifa home. "I was one of the officers whose duty it was to inform families that a loved one had fallen in battle. We were always three—usually an officer, a physician and a lawyer, all in uniform. There had to be one officer. The physician went along in case somebody collapsed. I didn't go along as a lawyer but as one who had experienced human contact in his work, and so could be helpful. We lawyers proposed this more personal approach because an officer might be too blunt.

"It was awful. We had casualties who were husbands, fathers, only sons or daughters. It was simply terrible. When people saw the three of us coming down the street they usually guessed at once.

"We inquired about the family beforehand and spent several hours seeing relatives, friends and neighbors to find out the best way to approach them. It was terribly hard. But afterwards we felt we had helped.

"There were many reactions to the news we brought. Some wept, some shouted, some wanted to commit suicide in our presence. Some listened calmly. You couldn't make any rules. Religious people took it well, as if saying, 'This is something from God. We can't change it.' Maybe it was easiest for them."

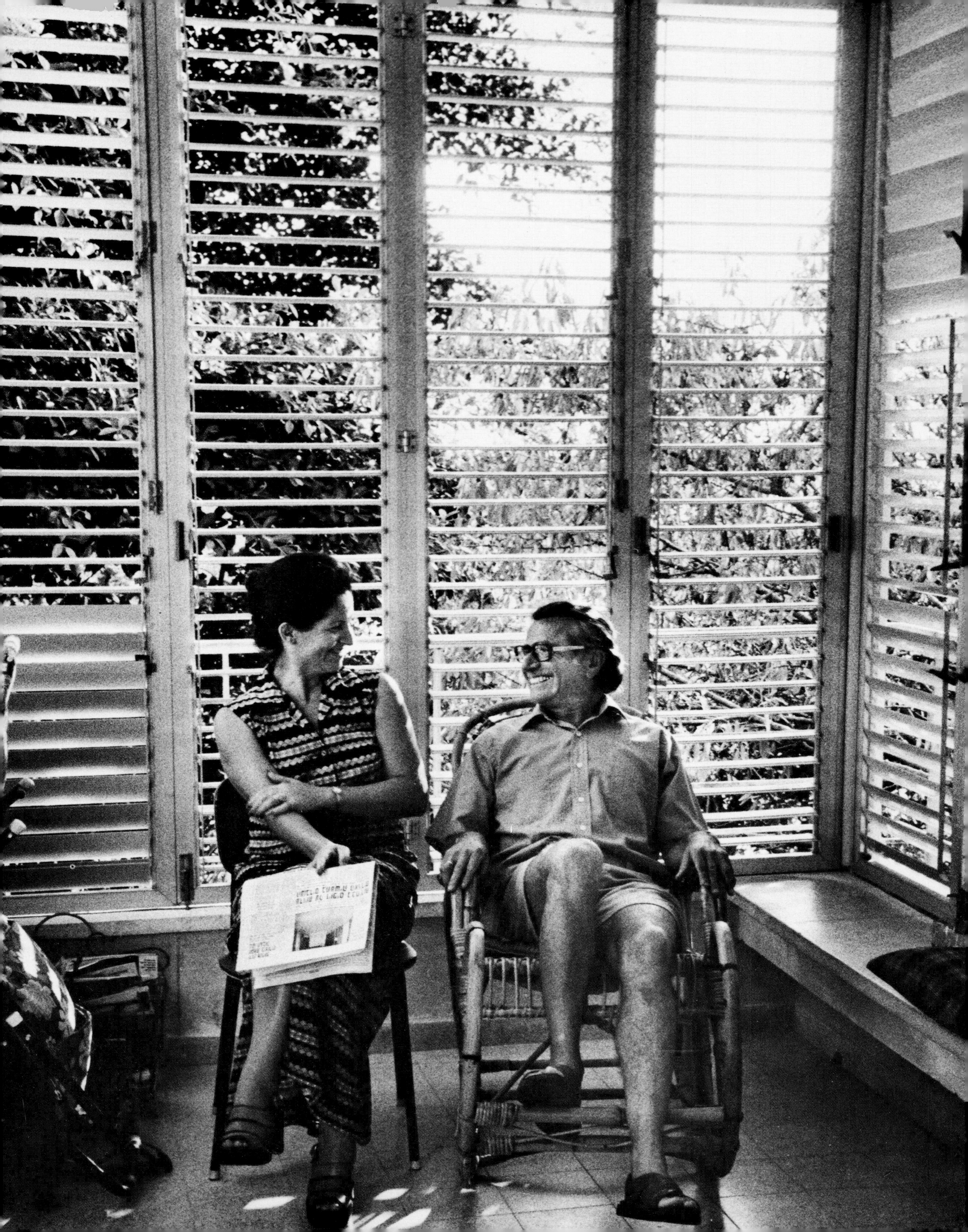

Uri Malul was just fourteen at the time of the siege of the Old City. Whenever I look back at the pictures of the refugees flowing through Zion Gate, I am struck by the resigned expression on the face of this teenage boy. I find it as profoundly affecting today as I did a quarter of a century ago. Uri was then a dispatch-bearer running messages from post to post, often under fire. In subsequent conflicts—the Canal War, the Six Day War—he served in the Tank Corps. "I'm too old to be called up again," Uri said in 1973. But he was mistaken. He was drafted on the sixth day of the Yom Kippur War. On the eighth day, Uri Malul, who had fought in every one of his country's wars, was killed in action at the age of thirty-nine.

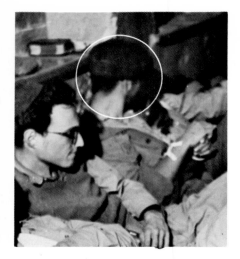

Rabbi Shear Yashuv Cohen, now the Chief Rabbi of Haifa, was assigned to the Jewish Quarter shortly before the British mandate ended. The Haganah wanted him to take charge of educational matters. In those last agonizing days of the mandate, the short drive from the New City to the Old was made by convoy. Twice a week army convoys took doctors, schoolteachers and medical supplies to the Jewish Quarter, which was already besieged by the Arabs. Some drivers were willing to smuggle members of the Haganah into the Jewish Quarter. The black market rate was five pounds a head, for the mandate authorities were determined to keep activists out of the quarter. The rendezvous was near the American consulate. Rabbi Cohen was picked up there one evening and dropped off at Zion Gate. He faded into the night. Nineteen years later during the Six Day War Rabbi Cohen was back in the Jewish Quarter. Within two hours of its liberation, he prayed at the Wailing Wall. This time the rabbi did not have to be smuggled into the old walled city. He was deputy mayor of Jerusalem.

When I accompanied Rabbi Shear Yashuv Cohen, a towering figure in black, to the Wailing Wall, he said, "Jerusalem can serve as a meeting place for all humankind and all believers of different nations and denominations and religions because the basic message of the prophets was that Jerusalem would become such a place. As I've said, things you love and admire can either bind you or make you enemies. Unfortunately the historical precedent has been that religions divided people; their beliefs would make men fight each other. I think it is a sign of the days to come that we are reaching an era when people will get close to each other. The connections are much easier. I hope this will bring understanding, and I believe that Jerusalem will play a major role in this trend.

"In a way it will be a spiritual capital in which the three big monotheistic religions can believe. I regard the Jewish religion as the mother of the other two. Of course, I maintain Jewish tradition and Jewish law and I think it's the right one. I still think that we all have many basic things in common which we should develop. And this will be the beginning of real peace.

"It's an amazing fact—you come to the Wailing Wall, the holiest place for the Jewish religion in the western world, and you find that the Jews pray on one side of it, the Moslems on top of the hill, and when you look from the hill you see the Holy Sepulchre of the Christians. It is all within two acres of land.

"If you start thinking about it, there is something that binds these people to this place—and Jerusalem binds all of these people. Historically this city has been the source of misunderstanding. Jerusalem could be the cradle of understanding."

John Phillips

Afterword by Teddy Kollek

History shows us that Jerusalem is a city that will never go under. Someone may destroy part of it; it will be rebuilt. Someone may kill or exile its inhabitants; others will take their place, or those who have been driven out will come back and rebuild it themselves. This book captures the vitality of Jerusalem and the vitality of the Jews. This is the Jews' city, and whenever they have the chance they return and rebuild it. They put into it all their effort, all their money, all their love.

This is a city that survives. It is difficult to survive in this world, and it is difficult for Jews to survive in this world. There is some heroism involved.

The people in these pictures, beleaguered in the Jewish Quarter of the Old City during the war in 1948, fought valiantly for a very long time. They were heroes of the struggle for Israel. Attempts to send them reinforcements failed. Finally, after weeks of siege and battle, they surrendered—only because they were told to by the people outside. There was no longer any hope.

This is the moment that John Phillips photographed: the last day that the Jewish Quarter existed and the end of the battle for the Old City. In a way, these pictures are a report from a kind of modern Josephus Flavius with a camera giving us a record of the final hours of Jewish courage. The next day the women were sent across the lines, the men were taken as prisoners of war, and the looting and destruction started.

I had first seen the Jewish Quarter in 1935, and saw it a few times after that in the thirties and forties. I saw it next in 1967 when we reunited the city; the shooting was still going on. I was then already the mayor of Jerusalem and was, of course, deeply disturbed by what had been done to the Jewish Quarter. To me there was obviously only one course: It had to be restored in good taste, and as many as possible of the families who had lived there had to be returned. That was the course we followed.

There is no reason to be squeamish about this: When the Arabs destroy something willfully, they leave it destroyed as a witness. We come back and, like ants, try to rebuild it. When the Arabs simply neglect something, we come back and restore it. After the Turks had cut down the trees around Jerusalem for fuel in the First World War, the Arabs never allowed the trees to grow again. They had a goat economy and the goats ate the tops of the little trees. When we came, we made them exchange goats for sheep and planted trees in and around Jerusalem, as we did all around the country. In another generation or two the country will be reforested as it was five hundred or two thousand years ago. The Arabs were just subtenants and did not care very much about the property; now the real tenants have come back and we take proper care of this city that has had meaning for Jews for twenty-five hundred years.

We could not let the Jewish Quarter remain as I saw it in 1967. All the synagogues had been destroyed. The only ones remaining were those that had been built down into the ground. (When the Jews returned from Spain early in the sixteenth century, they were not allowed to build higher than the nearby Arab buildings, so they dug their synagogues as much as two stories into the ground. They were also fulfilling a Biblical verse that says "Out of the depths I cried out unto you, O Lord.") After 1948 these underground synagogues were covered over with rubble, and underneath, the empty shells were used as sheds for donkeys and goats. Some Arab families had lived in the Jewish Quarter for generations; by 1967 others, who were refugees from the 1948 war, moved into those empty shells of synagogues and found them at least better than the UN refugee camps.

We decided from the beginning to restore everything that was restorable and to rebuild to scale, and with stone, where we had to fill in. There were many arguments. Some people wanted to bring back as many Jews as possible and, therefore, to build high-rise apartments. We refused that. Some architects opposed the idea of rebuilding with stone. They said this was reactionary and that we should allow people to build with contemporary materials: glass and steel, concrete and plastic. We insisted on keeping the unity of the Old City with beautiful Jerusalem stone. We are talking about a very small area. The entire Old City is about 225 acres; the Jewish Quarter in its southeast corner is only 28¾ acres. That is the whole thing. These 28¾ acres include the area near the Western Wall with the Armenian Quarter to the west, the Moslem Quarter to the north, and the Temple area to the east. The only people living there since before 1948 whom we actually evacuated were 106 Arab families in adobe huts stuck up against the Western Wall. We wanted to make a plaza there in front of the Wall, because we knew that tens of thousands of people would want to come to this place. On Yom Kippur and the anniversary of the destruction of the Temple, more than fifty thousand people at the same time pray in this open square.

Another problem we had was that there were no clear property rights in the ancient Jewish Quarter. In some buildings the first floor belonged to an Arab, the second to a Jew, the third to a Christian. The only way to reconstruct the quarter was to expropriate all of it from everybody and to rebuild. In the process we had to remove about twenty families; we paid them compensation for what we took from them. This was not pleasant, but it was in no way comparable to the hardships suffered by the thousands of Jews who had to leave in 1948.

Our plan calls for about six hundred families and three residential religious schools in the Quarter—about thirty-five hundred Jews altogether, which is fewer than were living there in 1948, though now under better conditions. A few dozen Arab families will also continue to live in the Quarter.

And we decided that before we rebuild, we would allow the archaeologists to dig down to bedrock and find what existed there. It was a rare opportunity to uncover history. They found some astonishing things in the Jewish Quarter: evidence of Jewish settlement under the First Kingdom and thereafter. We found twenty-four-hundred-year-old Jewish coins with the Yahud inscription. We found Jewish symbols from the Byzantine period. We found in private homes and public buildings evidence of an elegant civilization during Herodian times.

We found very moving things. One house had obviously been burned and the roof had fallen in at the time the Temple was burned. We found one of the largest churches that had been built in ancient Christianity, the Nea Church, built under Justinian in the sixth century. And the most incongruous thing: the little church where the Order of the Teutonic Knights had been created in the twelfth century. No one had known exactly where this church had stood; it was covered by rubble and Arab-built houses. From there the German knights had gone on to win Prussia from the Slavs and become the backbone of the Hohenzollern kingdom and brought all that trouble on the world (lower right).

Our purpose is to protect all the history of our city, whether it is Jewish, Christian or Moslem. And we respect history, whether it is history we like or not. So the Jerusalem Foundation got some money from Germany and restored the outline of this little church and made a walled garden that you can walk through on the way to the Western Wall.

The first thing the Jerusalem Foundation tackled was the restoration of the four synagogues in the complex named for Yochanan Ben Zakkai, who was a sage in the time of the destruction of the Temple (upper right). These four Sephardic synagogues had been built next to each other when the Jews came out of Spain, and the Sephardic chief rabbi had his headquarters there until 1948. In 1967 we found them in ruins.

The largest synagogue in the Jewish Quarter was the Hurva, which was built two hundred years ago by the Solomon family. We plan to leave a corner of the ruins as a memorial to the destruction of the Quarter and rebuild a new Hurva synagogue one block away. We have also restored two old houses, called the Yishuv Court, and refurbished them to show how Jews lived between 1700 and the arrival of modern technology after 1917 (overleaf).

There have been Jews living in Jerusalem since 600 B.C.E., with only three interruptions. The first came in 135 C.E., when Hadrian drove out all the Jews and leveled the city. The second was in 1099, when the Crusaders slaughtered all the Moslems and Jews. When the philosopher and historian Ramban ben Nachman came to Jerusalem in the thirteenth century, he wrote back to Spain that he had found exactly two Jews living there. Since then Jews have lived in the Jewish Quarter of the Old City through all the centuries until 1948—the third interruption, which lasted nineteen years. But the Jews always come back. Nothing will stop them.

Teddy Kollek

Jerusalem
September 21, 1976

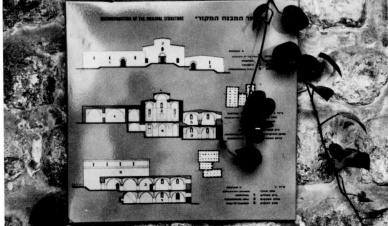